McCall's Illustrated Dinner Party Cookbook

McCALL'S ILLUSTRATED DINNER PARTY COOKBOOK

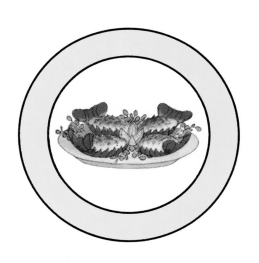  

By the Food Editors of McCALL'S

The McCall Publishing Company / New York

Published simultaneously in Canada by Doubleday Canada Ltd., Toronto.

Library of Congress Catalog Card Number: 73–106997

SBN 8415–0027–4

Drawings by Ginnie Hofmann, Werner Kappes, and John Woods

Printed in the United States of America

Contents

✾✾✾

Introduction

❈❈❈

A company dinner is a challenge to any hostess, especially the young homemaker who has had little experience in the kitchen. The menus and recipes in this book have been selected to help you prepare a wide variety of delicious foods with a minimum of worry and fluster. The step-by-step recipes, many of which first appeared in *McCall's* magazine in a series designed for the beginning cook, are simple to prepare yet interesting enough for the homemaker whose taste in fine food may be slightly beyond her skill in cooking.

Arranged by main course and featuring superb meat, poultry, and fish dishes, this cookbook provides a complete dinner menu for twenty-five different parties. The recipes include traditional favorites as well as foreign specialties and run the gamut of the menu, from tasty appetizers to mouth-watering desserts. As an added bonus there is a special section devoted to party desserts: The dessert recipes alone are sure to make your reputation as a hostess.

The menu ideas are suitable for practically every type of entertaining, ranging from informal get-togethers with friends and neighbors to elaborate dinner parties and bountiful holiday meals. Some menus lend themselves to impromptu dinners when friends drop by and there is no pretext of glamour; serving company merely requires an extra plate or two. Some menus are appropriate for out-of-doors dining; others for hot- or cold-weather meals. In special seasonal menus you will find ideas for table decor as well as practical advice on serving. In many of the menus alternates are suggested so that you may choose among several dishes. This feature will allow you to adapt the menu to your taste and to the time and energy you wish to spend. You may follow the menus exactly, modify them, or use them simply to inspire your own ideas.

All of the recipes have been tested in *McCall's* kitchens so that successful results are guaranteed; there is no need for guesswork. Each step in food preparation is so clearly explained that it is virtually impossible for any cook, even the novice, to go wrong. Moreover, the recipes are very practical for entertaining since many of the dishes may be made partially or entirely ahead of time. Even those dishes which may seem complicated are really not, because many of the steps in their preparation may be done ahead.

Of course, it is always preferable to have as little work as possible to do on the day of the party. That is why we cannot overemphasize the importance of planning ahead—it is the best way to ensure the success of your party. We also suggest that the inexperienced hostess keep the number of courses to a minimum until she has developed a repertory of dishes that she can prepare with ease and serve with confidence. In general today's menus are simpler since entertaining is more informal. The modern hostess serves fewer courses but strives to make the food more interesting—often one outstanding dish can transform an ordinary dining occasion into a memorable event.

We recommend that you give any new menu a trial run rather than serve a group of unfamiliar dishes for the first time to guests. Try the menu out on your family beforehand.

The Buffet

The informal dinner party at home is the most customary way of entertaining, but unless there is adequate help, the sit-down dinner is best limited to small groups. For dinner parties larger than six or eight, we suggest modified buffet service. Actually, this is a sit-down buffet where the guests first serve themselves from the buffet table, and then are seated at assigned places at a beautifully set dinner table.

In many of the menus we have included specific serving suggestions. As a general rule, when you have little serving help, it is a good idea to have the first course already placed on the dinner table before the guests sit down. Or serve the first course in the living room. On a cold night, for example, start your entertaining with steaming bowls of hot soup or a punch heavy with spices and heady with wines, served in front of a roaring fire.

If you do have someone to serve, that person will clear the

dinner table between each course and serve the dessert and coffee. If the dessert is an awe-inspiring creation or something very elaborate, it can be carried in for a dramatic effect and served family-style at the table. Afterward, serve the coffee and liqueurs in the living room.

A Word about Wine

Wine makes a unique contribution to the enjoyment of good food. Wine enriches any meal, even the simplest occasion when family or friends gather around the dining table. Yet since there are hundreds of wines—indeed, whole books have been written on selecting and serving wines—which wine to serve can be a rather complicated affair. For our purposes we will deal only with dinner (or table) wines and give you a few general rules. Just remember that your own taste is the best guide to food and wine combinations.

A red dinner wine usually accompanies red meat—steaks, chops, roasts, and game. It is also good with lamb, cheese, and spaghetti, as well as many highly seasoned casseroles. The red wines include Burgundy, Bordeaux, and Chianti. White wine is excellent with white meats (pork, chicken, seafood) and can be served with ham, veal, eggs, and light dishes such as soufflés. The white wines include Sauterne, Rhine wine, and Chablis. Rosé, a pink wine, is all-purpose. Some rosés go very well with seafood and other dishes for which white wine is generally recommended. Champagne, a sparkling wine, goes with everything too. Traditionally, it is served at gala occasions such as weddings, holiday meals, or special celebrations.

White and rosé wines are served chilled; champagne should be served very cold. Red wine is served at room temperature. The fragrance of a red wine is improved if the cork is removed an hour before serving, which gives the wine a chance to "breathe."

A wine bottle should be stored on its side, to keep the cork wet, so that it won't shrink and allow air into the bottle. Do not shake or jostle the bottle for a good hour before serving, to give the sediment a chance to collect and stay at the bottom of the bottle.

There are domestic wines and imported wines, with good wines and inferior wines in each category. Until you are able to choose wines by yourself, it is best to rely on the advice of a knowledgeable wine merchant or liquor store salesman. In most of our menus we have suggested a wine which complements the main course and which can be served throughout the meal. Whether you follow our recommendation or substitute your own favorite wine, make sure to have enough bottles on hand so that you can be generous with the wine service.

There are different types of glasses that are traditionally used with certain wines. An all-purpose wine glass should be of clear glass with a slim stem, its bowl tapering slightly inward at the top. The ideal all-purpose glass in which to serve wine holds about nine ounces. Wine will taste best if you fill the glass only one half to two thirds full. Space left in the glass permits you to enjoy the wine's aroma.

McCall's Illustrated Dinner Party Cookbook

A Christmas Holiday Dinner

The Christmas season is a time of warm hospitality and informal entertaining. Our dinner of traditional holiday favorites captures the spirit of the season.

At first glance this menu may seem rather complicated, but many of the dishes may be made partially or entirely ahead. The punches and the jellied consommé must, in fact, be prepared several hours ahead. The canapés may be made through step 3, then baked just before serving.

Our noble roast beef flavored with red wine requires a minimum of 3½ hours roasting time. While the roast is in the oven, prepare the Yorkshire pudding or the roast potatoes and the vegetables. Make the gravy for the roast, and put the finishing touches on the dinner.

Place individual cups of jellied consommé with red caviar at each place setting before the guests are seated. Carve the roast beef at the table and serve it family-style along with the accompaniments. At the appropriate time, carry the dessert to the table and serve it in grand style.

As for the dessert choices, the pudding may be steamed ahead and reheated for serving. The delicious cheesecake may be made the day before and refrigerated. Only the baked Alaska cannot be made in advance.

Decorate your table with fragrant evergreen and holly. Use a bright red or green cloth, and pewter combined with white ironstone for the serving dishes and dinner plates. And don't forget the red candles—they will add a gay and festive note.

A CHRISTMAS HOLIDAY DINNER
(Planned for Eight to Ten)

Frosty Daiquiri Punch
OR
Mulled Fruit Punch
Hot Cheese Canapés

Jellied Consommé with Red Caviar

Roast Beef
Yorkshire Pudding OR *Savory Roast Potatoes*
Buttered Peas with Mushrooms
Cauliflower with Shrimp Sauce

Hearts of Celery OR *Fennel, Cherry Tomatoes,*
Radishes and Scallions on Ice
Hot Rolls *Butter*

Steamed Fig Pudding
with
Hard Sauce
OR
Christmas Baked Alaska, page 54
OR
Glazed Lemon-Cream-Cheese Cake, page 58
Red Burgundy *Coffee*

2

Frosty Daiquiri Punch

Frosted Punch Bowl, below
1 bottle (16 oz) daiquiri mix
6 tablespoons superfine sugar
2½ cups light rum
½ cup curaçao or cointreau
2 dozen ice cubes
1 bottle (1 pint, 12 oz) club soda, chilled

1. Day ahead, prepare Frosted Punch Bowl.
2. In pitcher or bowl, combine daiquiri mix and sugar, and stir until sugar is dissolved. Add rum and curaçao.
3. Refrigerate, stirring occasionally, until well chilled—about 3 hours.
4. To serve: Place half of daiquiri mixture and 1 dozen ice cubes in electric blender; blend, at high speed, 15 to 20 seconds. Pour into punch bowl. Repeat with remaining mixture and ice. Stir in club soda.

MAKES ABOUT 20 (4-OZ) SERVINGS.

Frosted Punch Bowl

Beat 1 egg white with 1 tablespoon water. Use to brush a band about 1½ inches wide on outside of punch bowl, at top. Sprinkle sheet of waxed paper with granulated sugar. Roll edge of bowl in sugar, to frost it. Let stand at room temperature about 20 minutes; then roll in sugar again. Set aside to dry—3 to 4 hours or overnight.

Mulled Fruit Punch

1 cup sugar
12 whole cloves
2 (2-inch pieces) cinnamon sticks
6 cups grapefruit juice
3 cups orange juice
1 quart cider

1. In saucepan, combine sugar, ½ cup water, the cloves, and cinnamon; bring to boiling. Reduce heat, and simmer 20 minutes. Strain.
2. In large bowl, combine fruit juices and cider; mix well. Stir in sugar syrup.
3. Reheat, and serve hot. This punch is also very good chilled. It may be made up to 2 weeks ahead, and reheated over and over, as needed. If desired, garnish with orange slices and cinnamon sticks.

MAKES 26 PUNCH-CUP SERVINGS.

Hot Cheese Canapés

2 eggs
1 cup finely grated Cheddar cheese
2 teaspoons grated onion or onion juice
½ teaspoon dry mustard
6 slices white bread
24 (1-inch) bacon squares

1. Preheat oven to 375F.
2. In small bowl, beat eggs with fork. Add grated cheese, onion, and the dry mustard; stir until they are well blended.
3. Trim crust from bread; cut each slice into quarters, to make 24 squares in all. Arrange in shallow baking pan. Spoon heaping teaspoonful cheese mixture on center of each bread square. Top each with a piece of bacon.
4. Bake 15 minutes, or until bread is toasted and topping is slightly puffed.

MAKES 2 DOZEN.

Jellied Consommé with Red Caviar

1 env unflavored gelatine
4 cans (10½-oz size) condensed beef consommé, undiluted (not chilled)
½ cup heavy cream, whipped
1 jar (4 oz) red caviar

1. In small saucepan, sprinkle gelatine over 1 cup consommé, to soften—2 to 3 minutes. Heat over low heat, stirring constantly, until gelatine is dissolved.
2. Turn into a 13-by-9-by-2-inch baking pan or 3-quart shallow baking dish. Add remaining consommé, stirring until well mixed.
3. Refrigerate until firm—at least 4 hours.
4. At serving time, cut consommé into about ½-inch cubes. Remove from pan with spatula, and place in bouillon cups or sherbet glasses. Spoon a heaping tablespoonful whipped cream on each serving. Sprinkle red caviar over cream. If desired, serve consommé in a large bowl set in ice.

MAKES 8 TO 10 SERVINGS.

Cauliflower with Shrimp Sauce

2 heads cauliflower (2 lb each)
2 tablespoons lemon juice
2 teaspoons salt
1 can (10 oz) frozen condensed cream-of-shrimp soup
½ cup light cream
½ cup tomato juice

1. Trim leaves and stems from cauliflower; wash thoroughly. Make two ½-inch-deep gashes across stems. Brush tops with lemon juice.
2. Place cauliflower, stem ends down, on rack in shallow roasting pan. Add enough water to just cover stems. Add salt to water.
3. Bring to boiling; steam gently, covered, 40 to 45 minutes, or until stems of cauliflower are tender. (Use sheet of foil if pan has no cover.)
4. Meanwhile, place unopened can of soup in hot water for 10 minutes. Turn soup into medium saucepan.
5. Stir in cream and tomato juice; bring to boiling, stirring frequently. Keep warm.
6. Drain cauliflower very well; place in heated serving dish. Spoon sauce over top.

MAKES 8 TO 10 SERVINGS.

Savory Roast Potatoes

½ cup butter or margarine
8 large baking potatoes (about 4 lb)
1 tablespoon seasoned salt
½ cup chicken broth

1. Preheat oven to 350F. Melt butter in a 13-by-9-by-1¾-inch baking pan.
2. Pare potatoes; roll in melted butter, to coat well. Sprinkle with seasoned salt.
3. Bake, uncovered, 1 hour. Remove pan from oven; turn potatoes. Add chicken broth.
4. Bake 1 hour longer, turning several times.

MAKES 8 SERVINGS.

Steamed Fig Pudding

2 cups sifted all-purpose flour
1 teaspoon baking soda
½ teaspoon salt
1 teaspoon cinnamon
¼ teaspoon nutmeg
¼ teaspoon cloves
¼ cup butter or margarine, melted
⅓ cup light molasses
¼ cup orange marmalade
½ cup milk
1 pkg (6 oz) dried figs, finely chopped
½ cup dark raisins
Boiling water
Hard Sauce

1. Lightly grease a 1½-quart pudding mold with tight-fitting cover.
2. Sift flour with baking soda, salt, and spices. Set aside.
3. In large bowl, combine butter, molasses, marmalade, and milk. Stir in flour mixture, then figs and raisins; mix well. Turn into prepared mold; cover tightly.
4. Place mold on trivet in large kettle. Then pour boiling water around mold to come halfway up side.
5. Cover kettle; bring to boiling. Reduce heat; boil gently 2¼ to 2½ hours. (To test for doneness: Cake tester inserted in center should come out clean.)
6. Remove mold to wire rack. Let stand 5 minutes.
7. With spatula, loosen edge of pudding from mold. Turn out on serving plate.
8. Serve warm, with Hard Sauce.

MAKES 8 SERVINGS.

Hard Sauce

¼ cup soft butter or margarine
1½ cups sifted confectioners' sugar
2 tablespoons light rum

1. In medium bowl, with portable electric mixer, beat butter until it is light.
2. Add sugar gradually, beating until sauce is smooth and fluffy. Beat in rum.
3. Refrigerate, covered, until ready to use.
4. Let stand at room temperature, to soften slightly, before serving.

MAKES ABOUT 1 CUP.

ROAST BEEF

½ teaspoon salt
¼ teaspoon dried
   marjoram leaves
¼ teaspoon dried
   thyme leaves
¼ teaspoon dried
   basil leaves
¼ teaspoon rubbed
   savory
⅛ teaspoon pepper
Standing 3-rib roast
   beef, bone in
   (8 to 9 lb)*
1 teaspoon liquid
   gravy seasoning
½ cup Burgundy

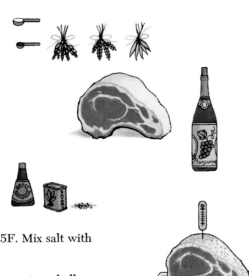

1. Preheat oven to 325F. Mix salt with the herbs and pepper.

2. Stand roast, fat side up, in a shallow roasting pan. Rub salt mixture into the beef on all sides. Insert meat thermometer through the outside fat into the thickest part of muscle (the point should not rest on fat or bone).

3. Mix gravy seasoning with Burgundy. Spoon some of mixture over the beef.

4. Roast, uncovered, basting several times with remaining Burgundy mixture, to desired doneness: rare (140F), 3½ hours; medium (160F), 4½ hours; well done (170F), 5 hours.

5. Get ready Yorkshire Pudding ingredients, at right, to assemble and bake when the roast is done.

6. Remove roast to heated platter. Pour drippings into a 2-cup measure. Let roast stand in warm place while pudding is baking and you're making Burgundy Sauce, at right. The roast will be easier to carve after standing 20 to 30 minutes. Makes 8 to 10 servings.

° Ribs that measure approximately 6 inches from chine bone to tip of the ribs. If ribs are cut longer, allow less roasting time. Diameter of roasts: 4 pounds, 4½ to 5 inches; 6 pounds, 5½ to 6 inches. Thinner roasts of same weight will require less roasting time.

YORKSHIRE PUDDING

2 eggs
1 cup milk
1 cup sifted all-
   purpose flour
½ teaspoon salt
2 tablespoons
   roast-beef
   drippings

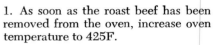

1. As soon as the roast beef has been removed from the oven, increase oven temperature to 425F.

2. In a medium bowl, with a rotary beater, beat eggs, milk, flour, and salt to make a smooth batter.

3. Pour drippings into a 10-inch pie plate; tilt to coat bottom and side of pie plate. Pour in batter.

4. Bake 23 to 25 minutes, or until the pudding is deep golden-brown. Serve immediately with the Roast Beef. MAKES 8 SERVINGS.

BURGUNDY SAUCE

6 tablespoons roast-
   beef drippings
¼ cup unsifted all-
   purpose flour
½ teaspoon salt
Dash pepper
2 cans (10½-oz size)
   condensed
   beef broth,
   undiluted
½ cup Burgundy

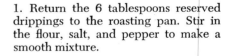

1. Return the 6 tablespoons reserved drippings to the roasting pan. Stir in the flour, salt, and pepper to make a smooth mixture.

2. Gradually add the beef broth and Burgundy to the flour mixture, stirring until it is smooth and browned bits in pan are dissolved.

3. Bring to boiling, stirring. Reduce heat, and simmer, stirring, 5 minutes longer. Taste, and add more salt and pepper, if necessary. MAKES 3 CUPS.

A Man's Favorite Dinner

If you are having cocktails before dinner, you may want to serve the guacamole dip with tortilla chips along with the drinks. Otherwise, the guacamole with crisp vegetables may be the first course salad.

Although this menu does require some last-minute work in the kitchen, it should be relatively simple to prepare since you are cooking for only four. A word of caution: Be careful not to overcook the London broil. Since flank steak is not the most tender cut of meat, it is best served rare. Also, be sure to slice the meat thinly on the diagonal, across the grain, which will make it seem more tender.

The apple dumplings, always popular with male guests, should be served warm, and topped with soft vanilla ice cream.

If your husband calls to say that he's bringing home two more friends from the office, you can easily expand the menu to serve six by increasing the amounts of the vegetables and the apple dumplings. The flank steak can serve six provided all of the guests do not have hearty appetites.

A MAN'S FAVORITE DINNER
(Planned for Four)

Guacamole with Crisp Vegetables

London Broil with Sautéed Onions
Maître d'Hôtel Butter Sauce
Perfect Baked Potatoes
Baked Tomato Halves

Hot Garlic Bread
Double-Chocolate-Almond Ice Cream
OR
Apple Dumplings, page 66
OR
Red Wine   Coffee

Guacamole with Crisp Vegetables

1 medium tomato, peeled	Chilled cauliflowerets
2 ripe avocados (about 1½ lb)	Crisp celery sticks
¼ cup finely chopped onion	Green onions
2 tablespoons finely chopped	Radishes
canned green chile peppers	Cherry tomatoes
1½ tablespoons white vinegar	Cucumber sticks
1 teaspoon salt	

1. In medium bowl, crush tomato with potato masher.
2. Halve avocados lengthwise; remove pits and peel. Slice avocados into crushed tomato; then mash until well blended.
3. Add onion, chile pepper, vinegar, and salt; mix well. Refrigerate, covered, until chilled. Serve at once or freeze.
4. To freeze: Place in 1-quart freezer container; place waxed paper directly on surface. Cover; seal; label, and freeze. Will keep a week.
5. To serve: Let thaw in refrigerator overnight. Place guacamole in bowl. Surround with vegetables.
MAKES 8 SERVINGS.

Maître d'Hôtel Butter Sauce

¼ cup butter or margarine, melted	½ teaspoon salt
1 tablespoon lemon juice	1 tablespoon finely chopped parsley

Melt butter, stirring, in small skillet over low heat. Remove from heat. Then stir in the remaining ingredients.
Serve hot or cold with London Broil.
MAKES ⅓ CUP.

Baked Tomato Halves

2 large tomatoes (about 1 lb)	½ teaspoon Worcestershire sauce
4 tablespoons butter or margarine	2 slices white bread, torn into coarse crumbs
¼ cup finely chopped onion	2 teaspoons chopped parsley
1 teaspoon prepared mustard	

1. Preheat oven to 350F. Wash tomatoes and remove stems. Cut in half crosswise. Place, cut side up, in small shallow baking pan.
2. In 2 tablespoons hot butter in small skillet, sauté onion until tender. Stir in mustard and Worcestershire. Spread on tomato halves.
3. Melt remaining butter in same skillet. Stir in bread crumbs and parsley. Sprinkle over tomatoes.
4. Bake, uncovered, 20 minutes, or until tomatoes are heated through and crumbs are golden-brown.
MAKES 4 SERVINGS.

Hot Garlic Bread

1 loaf French bread	1 teaspoon dried marjoram leaves
½ cup soft butter or margarine	¼ teaspoon pepper
1 clove garlic, crushed	Dash cayenne
3 tablespoons grated Parmesan cheese	

1. Preheat oven to 350F.
2. At 1-inch intervals, make diagonal cuts in loaf; don't cut through bottom.
3. In small bowl, combine remaining ingredients until well blended. Spread mixture between bread slices.
4. Place bread on ungreased cookie sheet; sprinkle top with few drops water.
5. Bake about 10 minutes, or until butter is melted and bread is hot. Serve immediately.
MAKES ABOUT 12 SERVINGS.

Double-Chocolate-Almond Ice Cream

2 pints chocolate ice cream	½ cup toasted unblanched whole almonds*
¼ cup chocolate syrup	
2 tablespoons crème de cacao (optional)	

1. If ice cream is very hard, place in refrigerator 30 minutes, or until slightly softened.
2. In chilled large bowl, combine ice cream, syrup, and crème de cacao.
3. With electric mixer or wooden spoon, quickly mix until combined. Mix in almonds.
4. Spoon into 1-quart mold, or return to cartons. Freeze, covered, until firm—at least 4 hours.
5. To serve: Unmold onto serving plate. Decorate with whipped cream and serve with chocolate syrup.
MAKES 6 SERVINGS.
*To toast almonds: Place in single layer in baking pan. Bake, in 350F oven, 10 to 12 minutes, or until skins start to crack.

LONDON BROIL WITH SAUTÉED ONIONS

London Broil

Perfect Baked
  Potatoes, at right
1 flank steak (about
  2 lb), or see note
1 tablespoon salad oil
2 teaspoons chopped parsley
1 clove garlic, crushed
1 teaspoon salt
1 teaspoon lemon juice
⅛ teaspoon pepper

Sautéed Onions

4 medium onions (¾ lb)
2 tablespoons butter
  or margarine
⅛ teaspoon paprika
⅛ teaspoon salt
2 teaspoons light-brown sugar

1. About 1 hour and 10 minutes before serving dinner, start Perfect Baked Potatoes.

2. With a sharp knife, trim fat from flank steak. Then wipe steak well with damp paper towels. Lay steak on cutting board.

3. In cup, combine salad oil, parsley, garlic, lemon juice, and pepper. Brush half of mixture over top of steak. Set aside.

4. About ½ hour before serving dinner, start Sautéed Onions: Peel onions, and slice thinly. Slowly melt butter in skillet. Add onion slices, paprika, and salt.

5. Cook over low heat, stirring occasionally, about 30 minutes, or until onions are nicely browned. Stir in brown sugar; cook a minute longer.

6. About 10 minutes before the onions are done, start broiling steak. Remove potatoes from oven; keep warm. Place steak, oil side up, on lightly greased broiler pan. Broil, 4 inches from heat, 5 minutes. Turn steak; brush with remaining oil mixture, and broil 4 to 5 minutes longer —the steak will be rare, which is the only way London broil should be served.

7. Place steak and onions on a board or platter; surround with the potatoes,

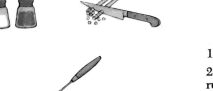

and, if desired, garnish with watercress or parsley.

8. To serve: Slice steak very thinly on diagonal, across the grain. Top each serving with sautéed onions. Or slice steak in the kitchen; arrange on platter; top with onions; surround with potatoes.

MAKES 4 SERVINGS.

NOTE: In many areas, in self-service meat departments, a cut of beef labeled London Broil (round steak) is sold. To prepare: While steak is still moist after being wiped with damp paper towels, sprinkle it with unseasoned meat tenderizer, as label directs. Then proceed as above, but omit salt from oil mixture. Since this cut is thicker than flank steak, increase broiling time 2 minutes per side.

PERFECT BAKED POTATOES

4 medium to large
baking potatoes
(about 2½ lb)
Butter or margarine
Salt
Pepper
Paprika
Dairy sour cream (optional)
Crumbled crisp bacon (optional)
Finely chopped green
onion (optional)

1. Preheat oven to 425F.

2. Scrub potatoes well under cold running water. Dry thoroughly with paper towels. With fork, prick skins over entire surface. (Brush potatoes with salad oil if you like skins soft after baking.)

3. Place potatoes right on oven rack, and bake 50 to 60 minutes, or until they are easily pierced with fork or feel soft when squeezed.

4. Slash an X in top of each potato. Then, holding potato with pot holders, squeeze ends so steam can escape and potato fluffs up.

5. Add a pat of butter to each; sprinkle with salt, pepper, and paprika. Or top with sour cream and bacon or green onion.

MAKES 4 SERVINGS.

For Friends or the Family

Here is a menu for a cozy winter evening at home, which can easily be expanded to accommodate an unexpected guest or two. The main dish, pot roast with vegetables, is a traditional favorite, and our recipe is distinguished by being particularly delicious.

Even if this dinner is only for the family, serve the first course, the cups of hot tomato bouillon (with an extra dash of sherry for the adults, plain for the children), in the living room before a roaring fire.

The pineapple upside-down cake is best served warm, right from the oven. This may require some last-minute juggling. To make your job easier, prepare the cake in advance through step 5 and refrigerate it. About 10 minutes before dinner is served, put the cake in the oven to bake and it will be ready for serving just about dessert time. Note: It may take slightly longer than the 45 minutes indicated if the cake has been refrigerated for an hour or more.

FOR FRIENDS OR THE FAMILY
(Planned for Six)

Hot Tomato Bouillon

Pot Roast with Vegetables
(Potatoes, Turnips, and Carrots)
Horseradish Sauce

Garden-Fresh Coleslaw
Assorted Hot Rolls   Butter

Caramel Rice Custard
OR
Pineapple Upside-Down Cake, page 56

Beaujolais   Coffee

Hot Tomato Bouillon

2 cans (10½-oz size) condensed beef bouillon, undiluted
1 can (13½ oz) tomato juice
1 can (10½ oz) condensed tomato soup, undiluted
1 tablespoon lemon juice
½ teaspoon salt
½ cup sherry

1. Combine all ingredients, except sherry, in large saucepan. Bring to boiling, stirring.
2. Stir in sherry. Serve.
MAKES 6 SERVINGS.

Horseradish Sauce

¼ cup butter or margarine
¼ cup flour
1 teaspoon salt
⅛ teaspoon pepper
1½ cups milk
¼ cup prepared horseradish, drained
1 tablespoon lemon juice

1. Melt butter in medium saucepan; remove from heat. Stir in flour, salt, and pepper until smooth. Gradually stir in milk.
2. Bring to boiling, over medium heat, stirring constantly. Reduce heat, and simmer 1 minute.
3. Add horseradish and lemon juice; reheat slowly, stirring.
MAKES ABOUT 1½ CUPS.

Garden-Fresh Coleslaw

1 head (2 lb) green cabbage, shredded (about 8 cups)
1 cup grated radish
½ large green pepper, chopped (½ cup)
½ bunch scallions, sliced (½ cup)
1 bottle (8 oz) coleslaw dressing
2 tablespoons milk
½ teaspoon salt
⅛ teaspoon pepper
Crisp lettuce

1. In large bowl, combine cabbage, radish, green pepper, and scallions. Add dressing, milk, salt, and pepper; toss until well blended. Refrigerate to chill well, several hours.
2. To serve: Line salad bowl with lettuce leaves. Turn slaw into bowl after tossing again to mix well.
MAKES 6 SERVINGS.

Carmel Rice Custard

⅓ cup raw regular white rice
5 cups milk
1 teaspoon salt
3 eggs
¾ cup sugar
1½ teaspoons vanilla extract

Caramel Syrup

⅓ cup sugar

1. Make custard: In top of double boiler, combine rice, 4 cups milk, and the salt. Cook over boiling water, stirring occasionally, 1 hour, or until rice is tender.

2. Preheat oven to 350F. Grease a 2-quart casserole; place in baking pan.
3. In a large bowl, combine eggs, sugar, vanilla, and remaining milk; beat just until blended. Gradually stir in hot rice mixture.
4. Pour into prepared casserole. Pour hot water to 1-inch depth around casserole.
5. Bake, uncovered, 50 to 60 minutes, or until silver knife inserted in custard 1 inch from edge of casserole comes out clean.
6. Remove from hot water to wire rack, and let cool. Then refrigerate until well chilled—at least 3 hours, or overnight.
7. About 1 hour before serving, make Caramel Syrup: In small, heavy skillet, over low heat and stirring constantly with wooden spoon, heat sugar until melted and golden. Remove from heat.
8. Using a teaspoon, drizzle hot syrup over top of custard. Refrigerate the custard until serving.
MAKES 6 TO 8 SERVINGS.

POT ROAST WITH VEGETABLES

3½-lb top- or bottom-round beef pot roast
All-purpose flour
Salt
Pepper
2 tablespoons
  salad oil
1 cup sliced
  onion
1 bay leaf
1 beef-bouillon cube
1 can (8 oz) tomato sauce
6 medium potatoes, pared (2 lb)
6 small white turnips, pared
6 carrots, pared and halved crosswise

1. Wipe roast well with damp paper towels. Combine 2 tablespoons flour, 1 teaspoon salt, and ⅛ teaspoon pepper. Sprinkle over entire roast, and rub into surface.

2. Heat salad oil in Dutch oven over high heat. Add roast, and cook, over medium heat, until well browned on all sides; turn with wooden spoons—takes 15 to 20 minutes.

3. When roast is partially browned, add onion, and brown very well. This is the secret of good flavor and color.

4. Add bay leaf, bouillon cube, 1 cup water. Reduce heat; simmer, covered, 1½ hours.

5. Turn roast. Add tomato sauce and vegetables, pressing them down into liquid. Simmer, covered, 1½ hours longer, or until roast and vegetables are tender.

6. Carefully lift out vegetables and roast, and arrange attractively on heated serving platter. Remove string. Keep warm.

7. For gravy: Strain pan liquid through a coarse sieve into a 4-cup measure, pressing any remaining vegetables through sieve. Tilt liquid; with tablespoon, skim off all fat.

8. Measure liquid, adding water, if necessary, to make 2½ cups. Return the liquid to the Dutch oven.

9. Measure ¼ cup flour into small bowl. Gradually add ½ cup water, stirring until smooth. Slowly stir into liquid in Dutch oven. Add ½ teaspoon salt and dash pepper. Bring to boiling, stirring constantly; reduce heat, and simmer 5 minutes.

10. Ladle some of gravy over meat. Pass rest, in gravy boat, with the roast and vegetables. Makes 6 servings.

From the Banks of the Danube

Here is a dinner with a Hungarian flavor that is sure to be appreciated by your guests. You may simplify the menu if you wish without changing its character.

In place of the galuska, the delicious tiny, old-world dumplings, you may substitute broad or medium-size noodles, cooked according to the package instructions, and tossed with melted butter and a few poppy seeds. (In this case, remember to omit the poppy seeds on the crescent rolls.)

For the deep-dish apple cider pie, you may substitute a store-bought cherry or apple strudel, or a frozen strudel that comes ready for baking. Serve the strudel warm and à la mode.

The other dishes may be prepared ahead, ready for last-minute heating and serving. The cheese spread and the cucumbers in dill improve on standing. The Hungarian goulash may be prepared through step 7. To serve, reheat it gently and add sour cream. The carrots may be cooked ahead, then reheated in the butter and sugar to glaze them before serving.

With or without the suggested substitutions this dinner is relatively simple to prepare, yet the menu is interesting enough for company.

FROM THE BANKS OF THE DANUBE
(*Planned for Six*)

Liptauer Cheese Spread
Assorted Crackers

Hungarian Goulash with Galuska
Braised Carrots

Cucumbers in Dill Dressing
Poppy-seed Crescent Rolls

Date-Walnut Squares with Whipped Cream
OR
Deep-dish Apple-Cider Pie, page 60
with Cheddar Cheese

Hungarian Wine or Beer   *Coffee*

Liptauer Cheese Spread

2 pkg (8-oz size) cream cheese, softened	1 tablespoon paprika
¼ cup soft butter or margarine	1 tablespoon snipped chives
1 teaspoon anchovy paste	¼ teaspoon salt
1 tablespoon prepared mustard	⅛ teaspoon pepper
½ teaspoon caraway seed	Garnish: Snipped chives, paprika, drained capers

1. In medium bowl, with portable electric mixer, beat cream cheese with butter, anchovy paste, and mustard until smooth and well combined.
2. Add remaining ingredients; mix well with a fork. Shape into a ball. Roll in more snipped chives.
3. Refrigerate, covered, to chill well.
4. To serve, sprinkle with paprika and decorate with capers. Place on board and surround with crackers.
MAKES ABOUT 30 APPETIZER SERVINGS.

Braised Carrots

1½ lb carrots	1 teaspoon sugar
1½ teaspoons salt	⅛ teaspoon pepper
3 tablespoons butter or margarine	1 tablespoon chopped parsley

1. Pare carrots. Cut lengthwise into thin slices, then into julienne strips.
2. In medium saucepan, cook carrots and 1 teaspoon salt in boiling water to cover, covered, 10 to 15 minutes, or until tender. Drain well.
3. Add butter, sugar, ½ teaspoon salt, and the pepper. Heat over low heat, gently stirring occasionally, 5 to 6 minutes, or until the carrots are glazed.
4. Turn into serving bowl. Sprinkle with parsley.
MAKES 6 SERVINGS.

Cucumbers in Dill Dressing

3 cucumbers	½ teaspoon salt
¼ cup snipped dill	Dash pepper
1 cup cider vinegar	Dill sprigs
2 tablespoons sugar	

1. Wash cucumbers; slice thinly into large bowl. Add snipped dill.
2. In 2-cup measure, combine vinegar, ¼ cup water, the sugar, salt, and pepper; stir until sugar is dissolved. Pour over cucumber; toss.
3. Refrigerate, covered, until well chilled—at least 1 hour.
4. To serve: With slotted utensil, remove cucumber to serving dish. Garnish with sprigs of dill.
MAKES 6 TO 8 SERVINGS.

Poppy-seed Crescent Rolls

2 pkg (8 oz) refrigerated crescent dinner rolls	1 egg
	Poppy seeds

1. Preheat oven to 375F. Shape crescent-roll dough, and place on cookie sheet, as package label directs.
2. In a small bowl, beat egg with a fork. Brush lightly on tops of rolls. Sprinkle crescents with poppy seeds.
3. Bake as package label directs, or until golden-brown.
4. Arrange in napkin-lined basket. Serve warm.
MAKES 16 ROLLS.

Date-Walnut Squares with Whipped Cream

¾ cup finely chopped dates	1 teaspoon vanilla extract
⅔ cup chopped walnuts	¼ teaspoon salt
3 tablespoons flour	½ cup light-brown sugar, firmly packed
1 teaspoon baking powder	
2 eggs, separated	½ cup heavy cream, whipped

1. Preheat oven to 350F. Lightly grease an 8-by-8-by-2-inch baking pan.
2. Place dates and walnuts in a large bowl. Sift flour and baking powder over them. Toss dates and walnuts, to mix well.
3. Add slightly beaten egg yolks and the vanilla: mix well.
4. In medium bowl, beat egg whites and salt until soft peaks form when beater is slowly raised. Add sugar gradually, beating until stiff peaks form.
5. With rubber scraper, fold into date-walnut mixture just until combined.
6. Turn into prepared pan; bake 20 minutes. Let cool in pan 10 minutes. Cut into 9 squares. Serve warm, with whipped cream.
MAKES 9 SERVINGS.

HUNGARIAN GOULASH WITH GALUSKA

Hungarian Goulash

¼ cup salad oil
3 lb boneless beef
   chuck, cut in
   1-inch cubes
1 lb onions, peeled
   and sliced (3 cups)
1 tablespoon paprika
1½ teaspoons salt
⅛ teaspoon pepper
1 can (10½ oz)
   condensed beef
   broth, undiluted
Galuska, at right
3 tablespoons flour
1 cup dairy sour
   cream

1. Heat oil in Dutch oven over high heat. Add beef cubes, in a single layer, and cook, over medium heat, until well browned on all sides. As cubes brown, remove to bowl. This takes about 15 to 20 minutes in all.

2. Add onion to drippings, and sauté until tender and golden-brown—about 10 minutes.

3. Return meat to Dutch oven. Add paprika, salt, and pepper, stirring until well blended with meat. Stir in ¾ cup broth.

4. Bring to boiling; reduce heat, and simmer, covered, 2 hours, or until beef is fork-tender.

5. Meanwhile, make Galuska.

6. In small bowl, combine flour and remaining broth, stirring until smooth. Gradually add to beef mixture, stirring constantly. Simmer, uncovered, and stir occasionally, 15 minutes longer.

7. Just before serving, place sour cream in small bowl; slowly add ½ cup hot gravy from beef. Slowly add to beef mixture, stirring until well blended. Heat, but do not boil. Serve

the goulash with galuska. Makes 6 servings.

Galuska

3¼ cups sifted all-
   purpose flour
3 eggs
Salt
2 tablespoons
   butter or margarine

1. In large bowl, combine flour, eggs, 1 teaspoon salt, and 1 cup water. Beat with portable electric mixer or wooden spoon until dough is smooth and bubbles appear on the surface.

2. In 4-quart kettle, bring 2 quarts water and 2 teaspoons salt to boiling.

3. To shape galuska: Spread a thin layer of dough (about 2 teaspoons) on pancake turner. Then hold over kettle of boiling water, and with moistened spatula cut off small pieces, letting them drop into water. Continue until one quarter of dough is used.

4. Boil gently, uncovered, until galuska are firm and rise to top of the water. Remove with slotted spoon, and place in colander or strainer. Quickly rinse with hot water; drain, and place in buttered casserole. Keep warm in 300F oven.

5. Repeat until all dough is used. When all galuska are cooked, toss them with the butter.

MAKES 6 SERVINGS.

NOTE: Or shape galuska as follows: Put half of dough at a time into a coarse colander. Holding colander over boiling water and using wooden spoon, press dough through holes. Boil, drain, keep warm as directed in step 4.

Come Autumn

This wholesome down-to-earth menu would be an excellent choice for an informal get-together in the fall, after the big football game, for example. It offers a happy combination of dishes, traditional favorites and some unusual ones, with interesting vegetables that are readily available in the autumn season and which make a decorative as well as a tasty contribution to the meal.

For your table use a rough, heavy linen cloth in a strong color, with napkins of a contrasting color, or a red- and white-checked tablecloth. Placemats of a sturdy fabric may be used if you want to expose the natural rough wood of the table top. Heavy earthenware or pottery pieces would be appropriate in this informal setting. Use several pots of chrysanthemums or red and white geraniums as your centerpiece.

COME AUTUMN
(*Planned for Six*)
Beet Soup with Dill

Beef Balls Stroganoff
Oven-steamed Rice
Herb-buttered Zucchini and Carrots
OR
Baked Yellow Squash

Beer Cabbage Slaw
Thin-sliced Pumpernickel Bread   *Sweet Butter*

Fresh-Apple Cake with Whipped Cream
OR
Old-fashioned Apple Pie, page 61

Red Wine or Beer   *Coffee*

Beet Soup with Dill

2 cans (1-lb size) julienne-style beets, undrained
2 cans (10½-oz size) condensed beef broth, undiluted
1 tablespoon snipped fresh dill
2 tablespoons instant minced onion
1 cup chopped raw cabbage
1 clove garlic, crushed
1½ teaspoons salt
6 tablespoons lemon juice
3 tablespoons light-brown sugar
Dairy sour cream

1. In a 6-quart saucepan, combine beets, broth, dill, onion, cabbage, garlic, salt, lemon juice, sugar, and 1½ cups water.
2. Over medium heat, bring to boiling. Reduce heat; simmer, uncovered, 15 minutes.
3. Serve hot, each serving topped with a spoonful of sour cream.
MAKES ABOUT 8 CUPS; 6 SERVINGS.

Herb-buttered Zucchini and Carrots

1½ lb small carrots
1½ lb small zucchini
½ cup boiling water
1 teaspoon salt
1 teaspoon dried thyme leaves
2 tablespoons butter or margarine

1. Scrub carrots and zucchini well with vegetable brush. Pare carrots. Slice carrots and zucchini, on diagonal, ⅛ inch thick.
2. To boiling water in 2½-quart saucepan, add salt, thyme, and carrots; bring to boiling, covered tightly. Reduce heat, and simmer 10 minutes. Carrots should be slightly underdone.
3. Add zucchini, tossing to mix well; bring to boiling, covered tightly. Reduce heat; simmer about 5 minutes, or until vegetables are tender. Let cook, uncovered, a few minutes longer, to evaporate liquid.
4. Add butter, tossing gently to coat vegetables.
MAKES 6 TO 8 SERVINGS.

Baked Yellow Squash

1 can (10½ oz) condensed beef broth, undiluted
2 lb yellow summer squash (about 3)
2 tablespoons butter or margarine, melted
½ teaspoon salt
1 teaspoon finely snipped fresh rosemary or oregano leaves*

1. Preheat oven to 350F.
2. Heat broth with 1 can water until thoroughly hot. Cut stem ends from squash. Cut squash in half lengthwise. Place halves, cut side down, in large, shallow baking dish.
3. Pour broth around squash; bake, uncovered, 20 minutes.
4. Turn squash; brush cut sides with butter combined with salt and rosemary.
5. Bake 15 minutes longer, or until squash is fork-tender. Before serving, brush with more butter, if desired.
MAKES 6 SERVINGS.
* Or use ½ teaspoon dried rosemary or oregano leaves.

Beer Cabbage Slaw

1 medium head green cabbage (2 lb)
1 large green pepper (½ lb)
1 to 2 tablespoons celery seed
1 teaspoon salt
¼ teaspoon pepper
1 teaspoon minced onion
1 cup mayonnaise
½ cup light beer

1. Shred cabbage and green pepper. Combine in large bowl with celery seed, salt, pepper, and onion.
2. In small bowl, combine mayonnaise and beer; blend well. Add to cabbage mixture; toss until well blended.
3. Refrigerate, covered, until well chilled—at least 3 hours.
MAKES 6 SERVINGS.

Fresh-Apple Cake

2 cups unsifted all-purpose flour
2 cups granulated sugar
2 teaspoons baking soda
1 teaspoon cinnamon
½ teaspoon nutmeg
½ teaspoon salt
4 cups finely diced pared raw apple (about 1½ lb)
½ cup chopped walnuts
½ cup soft butter or margarine
2 eggs
Confectioners' sugar

1. Preheat oven to 325F. Grease a 13-by-9-by-2-inch baking pan.
2. Into large bowl, sift flour with granulated sugar, soda, cinnamon, nutmeg, and salt.
3. Add apple, nuts, butter, and eggs. Beat until just combined—it will be thick. Turn into prepared pan.
4. Bake 1 hour, or until top springs back when lightly pressed with fingertip. Cool slightly in pan on wire rack. Sprinkle with confectioners' sugar.
5. Serve warm, cut into squares. Top with whipped cream or ice cream, if desired.
MAKES 10 SERVINGS.

BEEF BALLS STROGANOFF

1¾ lb ground
  chuck
1 teaspoon
  salt
¼ teaspoon pepper
4 teaspoons bottled steak sauce
⅓ cup packaged
  dry bread crumbs
1 egg
2 tablespoons butter or
  margarine

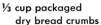

1. Make Beef Balls: In large bowl, lightly toss ground chuck with salt, pepper, steak sauce, crumbs, and the egg until well combined.

2. Using hands, gently shape the chuck mixture into 18 balls, each about 2 inches in diameter.

3. In 2 tablespoons hot butter in large skillet, brown beef balls well all over. Reduce heat; cook gently about 10 minutes. Remove beef balls.

4. Make Sauce: See ingredients, top right. To drippings in skillet, add 2 tablespoons butter. Sauté mushrooms 5 minutes, stirring. Then remove from heat. Stir in flour and catsup.

5. Gradually stir in broth. Add the onion-soup mix; bring to boiling, stirring. Then reduce heat, and simmer for 2 minutes.

6. Add beef balls; simmer gently 5 minutes, or until heated through.

Sauce

2 tablespoons butter
  or margarine
½ lb mushrooms, sliced
2 tablespoons flour
1 teaspoon catsup
1 can (10½ oz)
  beef broth,
  undiluted
½ pkg (1⅝ oz) dry
  onion-soup
  mix
1 cup dairy
  sour cream

7. Stir in sour cream; heat gently, over low heat. Serve over Oven-steamed Rice, below. MAKES 6 SERVINGS.

OVEN-STEAMED RICE

1½ cups raw converted
  white rice
1½ teaspoons salt
Dash of
  pepper

2 table-
  spoons
butter or margarine
3½ cups boiling
  water
¼ cup sliced green
  onions

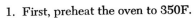

1. First, preheat the oven to 350F.

2. In 2-quart, ungreased casserole, with tight-fitting lid, mix rice, salt, pepper. Dot with butter.

3. Pour boiling water over rice; stir, with fork, to melt butter.

4. Bake, covered, 45 minutes (do not lift the lid). Add the green onions; mix lightly. To serve, fluff up rice lightly, with a fork, to mix well.
MAKES 6 SERVINGS.

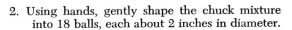

11

On a Wintry Evening

❀ ❀ ❀

This is the type of menu that is most appreciated by hostesses—it can be prepared with a minimum of worry and fluster. Moreover, once the meal is ready, it can wait almost indefinitely for late arrivals who have been detained due to traffic, weather, or because of an unpredictable spouse. This supper is also hard to beat for a company meal at which you'd like to have all the guests feeling relaxed and congenial.

Dinner can be served in about twenty minutes after the last guests have arrived. While the soup, sauerbraten, and cabbage are heating, the noodles can be freshly cooked.

The deep-dish peach pie, made from canned fruit if fresh peaches are not available, is waiting on the kitchen counter, ready for baking. Just pop it into the oven after the guests have arrived. This will give the pie ample time for baking and a chance to cool sufficiently before serving. The Dutch chocolate cake can be made early in the day. Serve dessert and coffee in the living room and look forward to an evening of stimulating conversation.

ON A WINTRY EVENING
(*Planned for Six*)

Stockpot Vegetable Soup

Sauerbraten wth Gingersnap Sauce
Red Cabbage with Apples
Caraway Noodles
Marinated Sliced Tomatoes
Corn Relish

Dark Pumpernickel Bread   *Sweet Butter*

Dutch Chocolate Cake
OR
Deep-dish Peach Pie, page 60

Red Wine or Beer   *Coffee*

Stockpot Vegetable Soup

2 cans (10¾-oz size) condensed vegetable-and-beef-stockpot soup
⅔ cup dry red wine
½ cup julienne carrot strips*
½ cup julienne celery strips*
½ cup fresh or frozen peas

1. In medium saucepan, combine undiluted soup with 2 cups water and red wine; heat to boiling.
2. Add vegetables; cook, covered, 10 minutes, or until vegetables are tender.
3. Ladle into bowls.
MAKES 6 SERVINGS.
° One inch; thin as matchsticks.

Marinated Sliced Tomatoes

4 large tomatoes
¼ cup salad oil
1 tablespoon lemon juice
½ teaspoon minced garlic
½ teaspoon salt
½ teaspoon dried oregano leaves

1. Peel and slice tomatoes. Arrange in shallow dish.
2. Combine oil, lemon juice, garlic, salt, and oregano; mix well.
3. Pour over tomatoes. Refrigerate, covered, 1 hour.
MAKES 6 SERVINGS.

Corn Relish

1 can (12 oz) whole-kernel corn
1 teaspoon mustard seed
½ teaspoon dry mustard
¼ teaspoon salt
¼ teaspoon pepper
⅓ cup cider vinegar
1 tablespoon salad oil
2 tablespoons light-brown sugar
½ cup chopped onion
2 canned pimientos, drained and chopped
¼ cup chopped green pepper

1. Drain liquid from corn into a small saucepan. Stir in mustard seed, mustard, salt, pepper, vinegar, oil, and brown sugar. Bring to a full boil.
2. Combine corn, onion, pimiento, and green pepper in medium bowl. Pour hot liquid over corn mixture; toss lightly until well combined.
3. Refrigerate, covered, at least 1 hour before serving.
MAKES 2½ CUPS.

Dutch Chocolate Cake

2 cups sifted all-purpose flour
2 cups granulated sugar
½ teaspoon salt
½ cup regular margarine
½ cup shortening
¼ cup unsweetened cocoa
2 eggs, slightly beaten
½ cup buttermilk
1 teaspoon baking soda
1 teaspoon cinnamon
1 teaspoon vanilla extract

Icing

½ cup regular margarine
¼ cup unsweetened cocoa
6 tablespoons milk
1 pkg (1 lb) confectioners' sugar
1 teaspoon vanilla extract
2 cups flaked coconut
1 cup chopped pecans

1. Preheat oven to 350F. Into large bowl, sift flour with granulated sugar and salt; set aside. Grease a 13-by-9-by-2-inch baking pan.
2. In small saucepan, combine ½ cup margarine, the shortening, ¼ cup cocoa, and 1 cup water; bring to boiling. Pour over flour mixture.
3. Add eggs, buttermilk, soda, cinnamon, and 1 teaspoon vanilla; with portable electric mixer, beat just until smooth. Immediately pour into prepared pan.
4. Bake 40 to 45 minutes, or until surface springs back when gently pressed with fingertip.
5. Meanwhile, make Icing: In medium saucepan, combine margarine, cocoa, and milk; bring just to boiling. Remove from heat.
6. Add sugar and vanilla; with spoon, beat until smooth. Stir in coconut and nuts. Spread over hot cake as soon as it is removed from oven. Cool in pan on wire rack.
MAKES 15 SERVINGS.

SAUERBRATEN WITH GINGERSNAP SAUCE

1 cup cider vinegar
1 cup Burgundy
2 onions, sliced
1 carrot, sliced
1 stalk celery,
chopped
2 whole allspice
4 whole cloves
1 tablespoon salt
1½ teaspoons pepper
3-lb boned chuck
pot roast
⅓ cup salad oil
4 tablespoons
unsifted all-
purpose flour
1 tablespoon sugar
½ cup crushed
gingersnaps

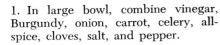

1. In large bowl, combine vinegar, Burgundy, onion, carrot, celery, allspice, cloves, salt, and pepper.

2. Wipe meat with damp cloth. Put meat in marinade; refrigerate, covered, for 3 days. Turn meat occasionally.

3. Remove meat from the marinade; wipe it dry with paper towels.

4. Heat Dutch oven. Add oil; heat.

5. Dredge meat in 2 tablespoons flour; in hot oil, brown very well on all sides.

6. Pour in marinade; simmer, covered, 2½ hours, or until meat is tender.

7. Remove meat from Dutch oven. Press liquid and vegetables through coarse sieve; skim off fat. Measure 3½ cups liquid (add water, if necessary). Return liquid to Dutch oven.

8. In small bowl, make paste of ⅓ cup cold water, remaining 2 tablespoons flour, and the sugar. Stir into liquid; bring to boiling, stirring. Add the crushed gingersnaps.

9. Return meat to the Dutch oven; simmer, covered, for 15 minutes. (If gravy seems too thick, add about ¼ cup water.)

10. Remove meat to heated platter; pour on some gravy. Serve, sliced thin, with more gravy. MAKES 6 SERVINGS.

Red Cabbage with Apples

1 medium head red
cabbage
2 tart red cooking
apples
2 tablespoons salt
2 tablespoons butter
or margarine
½ cup cider vinegar
½ cup sugar
1 tablespoon flour

Caraway Noodles

1 tablespoon salt
3 quarts water
1 pkg (8 oz) medium
noodles
¼ cup melted butter
or margarine
1 tablespoon
caraway seed

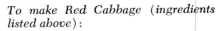

To make Red Cabbage (ingredients listed above):

1. Remove outer leaves from cabbage. Cut cabbage into quarters; discard core. Shred cabbage; measure 10 cups.

2. Core the apples; slice them thinly, but do not pare.

3. In large skillet, combine cabbage, apples, salt, butter, vinegar, sugar, and ½ cup cold water.

4. Cook, covered, over medium heat, stirring occasionally, 20 to 25 minutes, or until the cabbage is tender but is still crisp.

5. Sprinkle flour over cabbage; mix well. Cook, stirring, until mixture thickens. MAKES 6 SERVINGS.

To make Caraway Noodles (ingredients listed above):

1. In large kettle, bring salted water to a rapid boil. Add the noodles.

2. Bring back to boiling; cook, uncovered, stirring occasionally with long-handled fork, 7 to 10 minutes, or just until the noodles are tender.

3. Drain; return to kettle. Add butter and caraway seed; then toss lightly to combine. MAKES 6 SERVINGS.

A Spring Menu

What could be more appropriate for a dinner party in the springtime than a savory roast leg of lamb—young spring lamb, so delicate and tender.

This is a rather unusual recipe for roast leg of lamb. Since the bone is removed, the lamb requires less roasting time and is also much easier to carve. Cooked in the French manner, the lamb is roasted only until medium rare. For guests who prefer lamb more well done, roast the meat 15 minutes longer than indicated in the recipe and serve them the outside slices.

This elegant menu belies the amount of work required. Only the sauce for the lamb and the ratatouille, for example, need last-minute attention. Be careful to follow precisely the directions for cooking the ratatouille to avoid overcooking.

The crème-de-menthe-parfait pie is absolutely delicious; the fruit makes a simple and light dessert. You may also want to have some ice cream on hand if you are expecting children.

As a salute to spring, make an arrangement of forsythia or pussy willows or use whatever spring flowers are in bloom—jonquils, tulips, lilacs, crocuses—and place them in low white bowls in the living room. A bowl of flowers on the dinner table would make a lovely centerpiece too.

A SPRING MENU
(Planned for Eight)
Jellied Madrilène

Leg of Lamb, French-style
Browned New Potatoes
Mushroom Ratatouille

Salad of Spring Greens

Pineapple Shells Filled with Lemon Ice
and Fresh Pineapple
Fudge Brownies
OR
Crème-De-Menthe-Parfait Pie

Red Bordeaux Wine   *Coffee*

Jellied Madrilène

1 env unflavored gelatine	4 tablespoons dry sherry
3 cans (13-oz size) consommé madrilène	Lime or lemon wedges
	Dairy sour cream

1. Sprinkle gelatine over ¼ cup water in small saucepan, to soften. Stir in ¼ cup madrilène. Heat, stirring constantly, just until gelatine is dissolved.
2. In medium bowl, stir into remaining madrilène, along with sherry. Pour into 13-by-9-by-2-inch pan.
3. Refrigerate until firm—at least 2 hours.
4. To serve: Cut jellied madrilène into ½-inch cubes. Spoon into chilled serving bowl, placed in crushed ice. Or serve in individual chilled bouillon cups. Garnish with lime wedges and sour cream.

MAKES 8 SERVINGS.

Mushroom Ratatouille

2 medium green peppers (1 lb)	4 medium tomatoes (1½ lb), peeled and cut into wedges
3 medium zucchini (1 lb)	2 teaspoons salt
1 lb small mushrooms	
½ cup salad or olive oil	¼ teaspoon pepper
1 cup thinly sliced onion	2 tablespoons chopped parsley
2 cloves garlic, crushed	

1. Wash peppers; halve. Remove ribs and seeds. Cut lengthwise into ¼-inch-thick slices.
2. Scrub zucchini. Cut crosswise into ½-inch-thick slices. Wash mushrooms; cut in halves.
3. In ¼ cup hot oil in large skillet, sauté green pepper, onion, and garlic about 5 minutes, or until onion is transparent. With slotted spoon, remove to medium bowl.
4. Add 2 tablespoons oil to skillet. In hot oil, sauté zucchini, turning frequently, until tender—about 10 minutes. With slotted utensil, remove from skillet to same bowl.
5. Add remaining oil to skillet. In hot oil, sauté mushrooms until golden—about 5 minutes.
6. Return vegetables to same skillet. Layer half of tomato wedges on top. Sprinkle with salt, pepper, and 1 tablespoon parsley. Stir gently just to combine.
7. Layer remaining tomato on top. Sprinkle with remaining parsley.
8. Simmer mixture, covered and over low heat, 10 minutes.
9. Remove cover; cook 5 minutes longer, or until liquid has evaporated.
10. Turn into large, shallow serving dish. Serve hot. Or refrigerate, covered, until very well chilled.

MAKES 8 TO 10 SERVINGS.

Fudge Brownies

½ cup sifted all-purpose flour	2 eggs
⅛ teaspoon baking powder	2 squares unsweetened chocolate, melted
⅛ teaspoon salt	
½ cup butter or regular margarine, softened	½ teaspoon vanilla
1 cup sugar	1 cup chopped walnuts

1. Preheat oven to 325F. Lightly grease an 8-by-8-by-2-inch pan. Sift flour with baking powder and salt.
2. In small bowl of electric mixer, at medium speed, beat butter, sugar, and eggs until light and fluffy.
3. Beat in melted chocolate and vanilla. At low speed, blend in flour mixture; with rubber scraper fold in chopped nuts.
4. Spread evenly in prepared pan; bake 30 minutes.
5. Cool 10 minutes. With sharp knife, cut into squares. Let cool completely in pan.

MAKES 16.

Crème-de-Menthe-Parfait Pie
Pie Shell

1¼ cups packaged graham-cracker crumbs	¼ cup butter or margarine, softened
¼ cup sugar	

Filling

2 env unflavored gelatine	⅓ cup green crème de menthe
¾ cup milk	¼ cup white crème de cacao
4 eggs, separated	1 cup heavy cream
½ cup sugar	Green food color
⅛ teaspoon salt	

1. Preheat oven to 375F.
2. Make Pie Shell: In medium bowl, combine graham-cracker crumbs and ¼ cup sugar. With a fork, mix in butter until well combined. Press mixture evenly on bottom and side of a 9-inch pie plate.
3. Bake 8 minutes, or until golden-brown. Cool completely on wire rack.
4. Make Filling: Sprinkle gelatine over milk in top of double boiler; let soften 3 minutes.
5. Add egg yolks, ¼ cup sugar, and the salt; beat with rotary beater or fork until well blended. Cook over boiling water, stirring constantly, about 5 minutes, or until gelatine dissolves and mixture thickens slightly and coats a metal spoon.
6. Remove double-boiler top from bottom. Stir crème de menthe and crème de cacao into custard mixture.
7. Set double-boiler top in bowl of ice cubes and water. Cool, stirring occasionally, 10 to 15 minutes, or until custard mixture is the consistency of unbeaten egg white.
8. Meanwhile, in medium bowl, whip cream. Refrigerate. Also, in large bowl, beat egg whites until soft peaks form when beater is slowly raised. Gradually beat in remaining ¼ cup sugar. Continue beating until stiff peaks form.
9. With rubber scraper or wire whisk, fold custard mixture into egg whites. Then fold in whipped cream and 1 or 2 drops food color until mixture is just combined.
10. Turn into baked crumb crust. Refrigerate 3 hours, or until filling is firm.
11. Decorate with more whipped cream, if desired.

MAKES 8 SERVINGS.

LEG OF LAMB, FRENCH-STYLE

6- to 7-lb leg of lamb
3 lb new potatoes, pared
¼ cup butter
  or margarine
2 carrots, pared, diced
1 cup diced celery,
  with leaves
1 small onion, peeled
  and diced
Dash thyme
2 bay leaves
2 cloves garlic,
  peeled and crushed
¾ cup red wine
1 teaspoon salt
⅛ teaspoon pepper

1. Have your meatman bone the leg of lamb and trim the shank. Do not have it rolled and tied.

2. Preheat oven to 500F. Place lamb flat, fat side down, in a shallow roasting pan. Arrange potatoes around meat; dot with butter. Roast, uncovered, 20 minutes.

3. Reduce oven temperature to 400F. Turn lamb fat side up; turn potatoes. Sprinkle carrots, celery, onion, thyme, bay leaves, and garlic over and around lamb. Roast, turning potatoes occasionally, 35 to 40 minutes longer —lamb will be medium rare.

4. Remove lamb and potatoes to serving platter. Keep warm.

5. Pour drippings into 1-cup measure, leaving vegetables in pan. Skim off all fat; discard. Return remaining drippings to pan. Add ½ cup water, the wine, salt, and pepper.

6. Bring to boiling; lower heat; simmer, uncovered, 3 minutes. Discard bay leaves. Press vegetables and juice through strainer into gravy boat.

7. To serve: Slice the leg of lamb crosswise. Pass the gravy.

MAKES 8 SERVINGS.

PINEAPPLE SHELLS FILLED WITH LEMON ICE AND FRESH PINEAPPLE

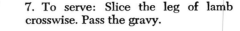

1 large ripe
  pineapple
¼ cup confectioners'
  sugar
1 quart lemon
  or pineapple ice
  or sherbet
About ¼ cup green
  crème de menthe
Fresh mint leaves

1. With a long-bladed, sharp knife, cut pineapple in half, right through the frond. With scissors, snip off the tips of the pineapple frond, if desired.

2. Remove pineapple from shells: With small, sharp knife, cut, on an angle, ¼ inch from edge of pineapple, to loosen meat. Then cut in half lengthwise, and remove sections. Refrigerate the shells.

3. Cut core from pineapple, and discard. Cut pineapple into small chunks. Place chunks in a medium bowl; stir in confectioners' sugar. Refrigerate until it is well chilled—at least 3 hours.

4. To serve: Fill shells with chilled pineapple. Top with small scoops of ice (these may be prepared ahead and stored in freezer until ready to use). Drizzle 2 tablespoons crème de menthe over ice in each shell. Garnish with mint leaves. Serve at once, spooning from the pineapple shells to serving plates.

MAKES 8 SERVINGS.

In the Irish Tradition

The Irish are noted for their simple food, which is wholesome and satisfying. Anyone lucky enough to receive an invitation to your informal dinner party in the Irish style will have fond memories of the occasion.

If fresh oysters are available you may wish to serve them as the first course. Oysters should be served well-iced on the shell with halves of lemon and accompanied by a pint of Guinness. The alternate choice, the green cabbage soup, is quite good too, and an excellent choice for a cold winter's night.

As far as the main dish is concerned, there are several theories about Irish stew: some cooks think that it should consist only of lamb and potatoes. We, however, are of the other opinion, believing that the addition of carrots, onions, and turnips makes the stew even more hearty, even more delectable.

We must admit that there is no substitute for real Irish breads. The oatmeal bread is quite tasty, though, and will be a nice accompaniment to the main course.

IN THE IRISH TRADITION
(Planned for Six)

Fresh Oysters on the Shell
OR
Green Cabbage Soup

Irish Stew
(with Potatoes, Carrots, and Turnips)
Wilted Cucumber Salad
Warm Oatmeal Bread   *Butter*

Deep-dish Plum Pie with Custard Sauce
OR
Steamed Raisin Pudding with Irish Whisky Sauce

Guinness Stout   *Coffee*

Green Cabbage Soup

4 cups shredded green cabbage	½ teaspoon mace
2 tablespoons butter or margarine, melted	3 cups milk
1 cup grated pared raw potato	½ cup crumbled crisp-cooked bacon
½ cup finely chopped onion	¼ cup grated Parmesan cheese
2 tablespoons flour	2 tablespoons finely chopped parsley
1 teaspoon salt	
¼ teaspoon pepper	

1. In ½ inch boiling water in large saucepan, cook cabbage, covered, 5 minutes; drain well.
2. Add butter, potato, onion, and flour. Cook, stirring, over low heat, 3 to 4 minutes—do not brown.
3. Add salt, pepper, mace, milk, and 2 cups water; bring to boiling. Reduce heat; simmer, covered, 20 minutes, or until vegetables are very tender.
4. Blend soup, a third at a time, in electric blender, covered and at high speed, 1½ minutes. Remove soup to saucepan after each blending.
5. Reheat gently, stirring. Add bacon, cheese, and parsley. MAKES ABOUT 1½ QUARTS.

Wilted Cucumber Salad

4 large cucumbers (2½ lb)	½ teaspoon white pepper
2 tablespoons salt	2 tablespoons snipped fresh dill or parsley
1 cup white vinegar	
¼ cup sugar	

1. Scrub cucumbers with vegetable brush; wipe dry with paper towels. Do not pare. Cut into thin slices.
2. In medium bowl, lightly toss cucumber with salt. Cover with a plate, and weight down with a heavy can. Let stand at room temperature 2 hours.
3. Drain cucumber well; pat dry with paper towels. Return to medium bowl.
4. In small bowl, combine vinegar, sugar, and pepper; mix well. Pour over cucumber slices. Refrigerate, covered, until well chilled—at least 4 hours or overnight.
5. To serve: Drain cucumber slices well. Turn into serving dish. Sprinkle with dill. MAKES 6 TO 8 SERVINGS.

Oatmeal Bread

3 cups sifted all-purpose flour	¼ cup honey
1¼ cups quick rolled oats	1½ cups milk
1½ tablespoons baking powder	1 tablespoon butter or margarine
2 teaspoons salt	
1 egg	

1. Preheat oven to 350F. Grease well a 9½-by-5¼-by-3-inch loaf pan; set aside.
2. In a large bowl, mix flour, oats, baking powder, and salt.
3. In a medium bowl, using rotary beater, beat egg with honey and milk, to mix well.
4. Pour egg mixture into the oats mixture; stir with a wooden spoon just until dry ingredients are moistened—mixture won't be smooth.
5. Spread batter in prepared pan. Bake 1 hour and 15 minutes, or until it is crusty and cake tester inserted in center comes out clean.
6. Turn loaf out of pan on wire rack. While loaf is still warm, brush top with 1 tablespoon melted butter. MAKES 1 LOAF.

Steamed Raisin Pudding with Irish Whisky Sauce

1½ cups milk	½ teaspoon cinnamon
1½ cups dark raisins, chopped	3 eggs
1½ cups sifted all-purpose flour	1½ cups fresh bread crumbs
2½ teaspoons baking powder	1 cup grated suet
⅔ cup sugar	Boiling water
½ teaspoon salt	Irish Whisky Sauce, above
1 teaspoon nutmeg	

1. In top of double boiler, over hot water, heat the milk and the chopped raisins 20 minutes.
2. Meanwhile, sift flour with baking powder, sugar, salt, nutmeg, and cinnamon; set aside.
3. In large bowl, with rotary beater, beat eggs until light. Beat in crumbs till well mixed. Beat in suet.
4. With wooden spoon, beat dry ingredients into egg mixture alternately with milk mixture, beating until well combined.
5. Turn into lightly greased 2-quart pudding mold; cover tightly. Place on trivet in large kettle; add enough boiling water to come half-way up side of mold.
6. Steam (water in kettle should be simmering), with kettle covered, 2 hours.
7. Meanwhile, make Irish Whisky Sauce.
8. Remove pudding from water; let stand about 5 minutes.
9. Turn out of mold. Serve warm, with sauce. MAKES 10 SERVINGS.
NOTE: Refrigerate any leftover pudding. Reheat for serving a day or two later.

Irish Whisky Sauce

¼ cup soft butter or margarine	1 cup light cream
2 cups light-brown sugar, firmly packed	Dash nutmeg
1 egg	¼ cup Irish whisky

1. In top of double boiler, with portable electric mixer at medium speed, beat butter with sugar until light and creamy.
2. Beat in egg, cream, and nutmeg; beat until mixture is fluffy.
3. Cook, stirring occasionally, over hot, not boiling, water until the mixture is thickened.
4. Remove from heat. Gradually stir in whisky.
5. Serve warm or cold, with pudding. MAKES 2½ CUPS.

IRISH STEW
(*with Potatoes, Carrots, and Turnips*)

2 tablespoons shortening
2½ lb boneless lamb, cut
   in 1½-inch cubes
1 tablespoon salt
⅛ teaspoon pepper
4 small white turnips (about ½ lb)
4 large carrots (¾ lb)
2 large onions (about ½ lb)
4 medium potatoes (about 1½ lb)
¼ cup instant-type flour
2 tablespoons chopped parsley

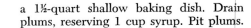

1. Heat shortening in Dutch oven over high heat. Add half of lamb cubes, and cook, over medium heat, until browned on all sides—about 10 minutes. Remove to bowl. Brown rest of lamb.

2. Return all meat to Dutch oven. Sprinkle with salt and pepper; stir in 3 cups water. Bring to boil; reduce heat; simmer, covered, 1 hour.

3. Meanwhile, pare turnips; cut crosswise into ½-inch-thick slices. Pare carrots; cut, on the diagonal, into ½-inch-thick slices. Peel onions; cut into quarters. Pare potatoes; cut into quarters. Place vegetables in plastic bag; set aside until meat has cooked 1 hour.

4. Add all vegetables to meat; return to boiling. Reduce heat; simmer, covered, 40 minutes, or until meat and vegetables are tender.

5. In small bowl, gradually stir ¼ cup water into flour until smooth. Slowly add to meat mixture, stirring constantly; boil gently 1 minute. Add parsley. MAKES 4 TO 6 SERVINGS.

Deep-dish Plum Pie
Custard Sauce, right, or light cream
or vanilla ice cream

2 cans (1-lb size) purple plums
1 tablespoon cornstarch
1 tablespoon lemon juice
1 tablespoon butter or margarine

Scone Topping:

1¼ cups packaged biscuit mix
½ cup quick rolled oats
¼ cup sugar
⅔ cup milk

1. Make Custard Sauce.

2. Preheat oven to 425F. Lightly grease

a 1½-quart shallow baking dish. Drain plums, reserving 1 cup syrup. Pit plums.

3. In a small saucepan, combine cornstarch with reserved plum syrup, stirring until smooth. Over medium heat, bring to boiling, stirring. Reduce heat, and simmer until mixture is thickened and translucent—2 minutes. Remove from heat.

4. Stir in lemon juice, butter, and plums. Return to medium heat, and cook 1 minute. Pour into prepared baking dish.

5. Make Scone Topping: In medium bowl, combine biscuit mix, oats, and sugar; mix well. Add milk, mixing quickly and lightly with a fork just until dry ingredients are moistened.

6. Drop topping by tablespoonsful over hot fruit; then spread with spatula, to cover fruit evenly and completely.

7. Bake 25 minutes, or until topping is golden-brown. Let pie stand on wire rack 20 minutes. Then serve with chilled Custard Sauce, light cream, or ice cream. MAKES 6 SERVINGS.

Custard Sauce

1 cup milk
2 egg yolks
2 tablespoons sugar
Dash salt
½ teaspoon vanilla extract

1. Place milk in top of double boiler; heat, over direct heat, until bubbles form around edge of pan. Remove from heat. Also, heat water in lower part of double boiler until very hot but not boiling.

2. In small bowl, with wooden spoon, lightly beat egg yolks with sugar and salt. Gradually add hot milk, beating constantly. Return to double-boiler top.

3. Set over hot water in double-boiler bottom, and cook 15 minutes, or until thin coating forms on a metal spoon.

4. Stir in vanilla. Strain custard into small bowl. Refrigerate, covered, until well chilled—at least 1 hour. MAKES ABOUT 1 CUP.

An Easter Buffet

Here is an impressive and unusual holiday buffet. Although the menu may look complicated, it is not difficult to prepare. In fact, many of the dishes may be prepared earlier in the day as follows.

Prepare the lettuce soup through step 2, so that it is ready to be cooked at serving time. The sweet potatoes, prepared in advance through step 4, need only to be reheated and flamed before serving. Marinate and refrigerate the leek and endive vinaigrette. Make the dessert in the morning. Unmold the frozen mousse on a silver platter and store in the freezer; decorate it before serving.

To facilitate your serving, have the soup on the dinner table before the guests sit down. Heat the artichokes and spinach at the last minute—when the soup is served. After the soup plates have been removed, let the guests help themselves from the buffet table. The host, of course, will carve the ham in crust for each guest.

The dessert, a very handsome mold with a garnish of whole fresh or frozen strawberries and candied violets, will be the *pièce de résistance*. The candied violets are imported from France and may be purchased at most speciality shops. A small box will be enough to garnish many desserts.

AN EASTER BUFFET
(Planned for Eight)

Cream of Lettuce Soup

Baked Ham in Biscuit Crust
Port Wine Sauce
Orange-glazed Sweet Potatoes
Artichokes Florentine

Cold Leeks and Endives Vinaigrette
Assorted Hot Rolls   Butter

Frozen Maple Mousse

Rosé Wine   Coffee

Liqueurs

Cream of Lettuce Soup

2 medium heads iceberg lettuce, or 1 large head romaine, shredded (about 8 cups)	¼ cup butter or margarine
	1 teaspoon sugar
	½ teaspoon salt
1½ cups chicken broth	⅛ teaspoon nutmeg
1½ cups light cream	Dash pepper

1. In 4-quart kettle, combine shredded lettuce and chicken broth; bring to boiling over medium heat. Reduce heat, and simmer, covered, 10 minutes, or just until lettuce is soft.
2. In electric-blender container, place one half lettuce and liquid; cover, and blend at high speed 1 minute. Pour into bowl. Repeat with remaining lettuce and liquid. Pour back into kettle.
3. Add cream, butter, sugar, salt, nutmeg, and pepper to mixture in kettle. Cook over medium heat, stirring, until butter is melted and soup is hot.
4. Beat mixture with a rotary beater, to make very smooth. Serve soup at once.
MAKES 8 SERVINGS.

Orange-glazed Sweet Potatoes

8 medium sweet potatoes (about 3 lb)*	½ cup orange juice
Boiling water	½ teaspoon salt
⅓ cup butter	½ cup slivered toasted almonds
1 cup brown sugar, firmly packed	⅓ cup brandy

1. Scrub potatoes. Place in large saucepan; cover with boiling water; bring back to boiling. Reduce heat, and simmer, covered, 30 minutes, or until tender.
2. Drain; let cool. Peel, and halve lengthwise.
3. Melt butter in large skillet. Add brown sugar, orange juice, and salt; bring to boiling, stirring until sugar is dissolved. Boil syrup gently 5 minutes.
4. Add potatoes, turning carefully to coat with syrup, heat 5 minutes. Sprinkle with almonds.
5. Heat brandy gently in small pan. Light with match; pour, flaming, over potatoes.
MAKES 8 SERVINGS.

* Or use 2 cans (1-lb-2-oz size) sweet potatoes; continue with Step 3.

Artichokes Florentine

2 cans (15-oz size) artichoke bottoms	2 pkg (10-oz size) frozen creamed spinach

1. In medium saucepan, heat artichoke bottoms in liquid from cans.
2. Heat frozen spinach as package labels direct.
3. Drain artichoke bottoms. Spoon spinach into artichokes.
MAKES 8 SERVINGS.

Cold Leeks and Endives Vinaigrette

Dressing

½ cup salad or olive oil	1 teaspoon sugar
2 tablespoons tarragon vinegar	¼ teaspoon pepper
1 tablespoon snipped chives	¼ teaspoon dry mustard
1 teaspoon salt	
2 bunches leeks (about 8)	1 teaspoon salt
3 Belgian endives, washed and crisped	Watercress sprigs

1. Make Dressing: In small bowl or tightly covered jar, combine oil, vinegar, chives, 1 teaspoon salt, the sugar, pepper, and mustard. Stir or shake until well blended. Refrigerate until needed.
2. Trim leeks: Cut off root ends and green stems—leeks should be about 7 inches long after trimming. Cut each in half lengthwise, being careful not to cut all the way through the root end. Wash throughly.

3. In 4-quart kettle, bring 2 quarts water to boiling. Add leeks and salt; simmer, covered, 15 minutes, or just until tender. Drain leeks.
4. Arrange leeks in shallow dish. Shake dressing well; pour over leeks. Refrigerate, covered, until well chilled—about 2 hours.
5. To serve: Remove leeks from dressing with slotted utensil, and arrange in center of chilled serving dish. Place endives, spoke fashion, at each end, and drizzle with dressing. Garnish with watercress.
MAKES 8 SERVINGS.

Frozen Maple Mousse

1¼ cups maple or maple-blended syrup	2 cups heavy cream
	Strawberries
2 egg yolks	Candied violets
⅛ teaspoon salt	Whipped cream (optional)

1. In top of double boiler, over direct heat, heat maple syrup just until it is bubbly around edge of the pan.
2. In small bowl, with electric mixer or rotary beater, beat egg yolks with salt until light-colored. Gradually beat in all the syrup. Return mixture to top of double boiler.
3. Cook over simmering water, stirring constantly, until mixture is slightly thickened and forms a coating on a metal spoon—10 to 15 minutes.
4. Set top of double boiler in ice water; beat mixture until thick and fluffy and well chilled—about 5 minutes.
5. In large chilled bowl, beat cream just until stiff. Fold in syrup mixture. Pour into 2 ice-cube trays.
6. Freeze until firm about 1 inch from edge. Turn into large bowl; beat with wire whisk until smooth. Turn into 6 cup mold, preferably with a tube.
7. Freeze, covered with plastic film, until it is firm—at least 4 hours.
8. To serve: Unmold onto chilled serving plate. Garnish with strawberries, candied violets, and whipped cream.
MAKES 8 SERVINGS.

BAKED HAM IN BISCUIT CRUST WITH PORT WINE SAUCE

Baked Ham

5- to 8-lb fully
cooked canned
or boneless
ham
½ cup cherry
preserves
2 tablespoons light
corn syrup

Port Wine Sauce

3 pkg (¾-oz size)
mushroom-gravy
sauce mix
1 cup port wine
½ cup cherry
preserves

1. Early in day: Preheat oven to 325F. Place ham, fat side up, on rack in shallow roasting pan. Insert meat thermometer in center. Bake 2 hours, or to 130F on thermometer.. Remove the thermometer.

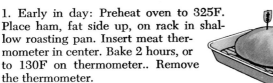

2. Combine ½ cup preserves and the corn syrup. Spoon half of mixture over ham. Then bake for 10 minutes.

3. Spoon on rest of mixture. Bake 15 minutes longer. Cool completely.

4. Two hours before serving, make Biscuit Crust. Mold around ham, and decorate as directed at right. Meanwhile, preheat oven to 325F.

5. Bake 1 hour, or till crust is golden. Let stand 10 minutes before slicing.

6. Meanwhile, make **Port Wine Sauce:** Make gravy as package label directs, using the port and 2 cups water and adding the ½ cup cherry preserves. Pass sauce with ham.

MAKES 10 SERVINGS.

Biscuit Crust

4 cups packaged
biscuit mix
1 teaspoon sage
2 tablespoons
prepared mustard
¼ cup soft
shortening
¾ cup water
1 can (4½ oz)
deviled ham
1 egg yolk

1. In large bowl, combine biscuit mix, sage, and mustard. With pastry blender, cut in shortening until mixture resembles coarse cornmeal.

2. Make a well in center; add water. Beat with a fork until combined. Shape into ball. Knead 5 minutes.

3. On a lightly floured pastry cloth, roll out four fifths of dough to 12-by-22-inch rectangle. Spread with deviled ham, leaving 1½-inch margins.

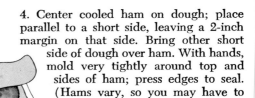

4. Center cooled ham on dough; place parallel to a short side, leaving a 2-inch margin on that side. Bring other short side of dough over ham. With hands, mold very tightly around top and sides of ham; press edges to seal. (Hams vary, so you may have to trim dough and patch, to cover the ham.)

5. Refrigerate the dough-covered ham on a greased cookie sheet.

6. Roll out rest of the dough ⅛ inch thick. With a sharp knife, cut out 18 holly-shape leaves.

7. Beat egg yolk with 1 tablespoon water. Brush dough evenly with some of egg-yolk mixture. Press leaves to dough; arrange decoratively. Brush leaves with rest of egg-yolk mixture. Bake as directed at left.

19

A Neighbors' Get-Together

This informal dinner menu for entertaining a group of good friends or neighbors has three appealing features: It is economical, easy to prepare, and will be appreciated by both adults and children.

This can be a practically effortless company dinner, something which the hostess will surely appreciate. Most of the meal can be prepared in the morning, which will allow you to spend time with your guests before dinner. The consommé, the ham loaf and mustard sauce, the macaroni and cheese, and the dessert may be prepared ahead to be baked or reheated in time for serving. If you know that your guests have less than robust appetites, you may omit either the macaroni and cheese or the cabbage wedges.

Both desserts are equally delicious. If you select the cream puffs, you can also fill them with strawberry or peach ice cream just before serving and use thawed frozen raspberries as the sauce.

A NEIGHBORS' GET-TOGETHER
(Planned for Six)

Hot Tomato Consommé

Glazed Ham Loaf with Mustard Sauce
Buttered Cabbage Wedges
Baked Macaroni and Cheese

Old-fashioned Lettuce Salad
Hot Cornbread   *Butter*

Butterscotch-Pecan Pie
OR
Cream Puffs, page 65

White Wine   *Coffee*

Hot Tomato Consommé

2 cans (1-lb size) tomatoes, undrained	12 whole black peppers
2 cans (10½-oz size) condensed chicken broth, undiluted	1 bay leaf
	1 tablespoon sugar
½ cup celery tops, cut up	Salt
4 sprigs parsley	Red food color
	Chopped parsley

1. Place tomatoes in large saucepan; crush with potato masher. Add chicken broth, 1 cup water, the celery, parsley sprigs, peppers, bay leaf.
2. Bring to boiling, stirring occasionally. Reduce heat, and simmer about 30 minutes.
3. Strain through a fine sieve. Add sugar, salt to taste, and a few drops food color. Keep hot.
4. At serving time, pour into mugs or soup bowls. Sprinkle with parsley.
MAKES 6 SERVINGS.

Baked Macaroni and Cheese

1 pkg (8 oz) elbow macaroni	⅛ teaspoon pepper
¼ cup butter or margarine	2 cups milk
¼ cup all-purpose flour	8 oz Cheddar cheese, grated
1 teaspoon salt	(2 cups)

1. Preheat oven to 350F. Cook macaroni as the package label directs; drain.
2. Meanwhile, melt butter in a medium saucepan; remove from heat. Stir in the flour, salt, and pepper until smooth. Gradually stir in milk. Bring to boiling, stirring. Reduce heat, and simmer mixture 1 minute. Remove from heat.
3. Stir in 1½ cups cheese and the macaroni. Pour into a 1½-quart casserole, and sprinkle remaining cheese over top.
4. Bake 15 to 20 minutes, or until cheese is golden-brown.
MAKES 6 SERVINGS.

Old-fashioned Lettuce Salad

2 quarts Boston or leaf lettuce in bite-size pieces	¼ cup lemon juice
	4 teaspoons sugar
½ cup sliced green onions	½ teaspoon salt
½ cup light cream	Dash white pepper

1. Place lettuce and green onions in salad bowl.
2. In small bowl, combine cream, lemon juice, sugar, salt, and pepper; mix well. Pour over lettuce, and toss well. Serve immediately.
MAKES 6 TO 8 SERVINGS.

Hot Cornbread

1 pkg (14 oz) corn-muffin mix	1 egg
2 tablespoons chopped parsley	1 cup milk
½ teaspoon dried thyme leaves	

1. Preheat oven to 400F. Grease an 8-by-8-by-2-inch baking pan.
2. In medium bowl, combine corn-muffin mix, parsley, and thyme.
3. Add egg and milk; mix just until dry ingredients are moistened.
4. Pour batter into prepared pan; spread evenly.
5. Bake about 25 minutes, or until light golden-brown.
6. Serve hot, cut into squares.
MAKES 9 SQUARES.
NOTE: You will need to bake the cornbread in a separate oven from the ham loaf and macaroni.

Butterscotch-Pecan Pie

3 eggs	2 tablespoons butter or margarine, melted
1 cup light corn syrup	
⅛ teaspoon salt	1 cup pecan halves
1 teaspoon vanilla extract	9-inch unbaked pie shell
1 cup sugar	Whipped cream

1. Preheat oven to 400F.
2. In medium bowl, beat eggs slightly. Add corn syrup, salt, vanilla, sugar, and butter; mix well. Stir in pecans. Pour into pie shell.
3. Bake 15 minutes. Reduce heat to 350F; bake 30 to 35 minutes, or until outer edge of filling seems set.
4. Let cool completely on wire rack. Just before serving, decorate with rosettes of whipped cream.
MAKES 8 SERVINGS.

GLAZED HAM LOAF

½ cup milk
1 egg
1 tablespoon catsup
1 tablespoon
  prepared mustard
⅛ teaspoon
  pepper
1 cup soft white-
  bread crumbs

1 lb ground ham
½ lb ground veal
2 tablespoons finely
  chopped onion
1 tablespoon
  chopped parsley

1 can (8¾ oz) fruits for salad
¼ cup light-brown sugar, firmly packed
2 tablespoons cider vinegar

Buttered Cabbage Wedges, below
Mustard Sauce, below

1. Preheat oven to 350F. In large bowl, combine milk, egg, catsup, mustard, and pepper; beat until well blended. Stir in bread crumbs; let mixture stand several minutes.

2. Add ham, veal, onion, and parsley; mix well. In shallow baking pan, shape meat into loaf about 8 inches long and 4 inches wide. Bake ham loaf, uncovered, for 30 minutes.

3. Meanwhile, make fruit glaze: Drain syrup from fruit into a small saucepan. Add brown sugar and vinegar; bring to boiling, stirring. Add fruit; reduce heat, and simmer 5 minutes. Remove saucepan from heat.

4. Remove ham loaf from oven. Pour glaze over loaf, arranging the fruit attractively on top. Then bake ham loaf 30 minutes longer.

5. Meanwhile, prepare Buttered Cabbage Wedges and Mustard Sauce, as directed.

6. With wide spatula, remove ham loaf to a warm platter. Spoon glaze from pan over top of the loaf. Surround the loaf with cabbage wedges, and pass mustard sauce separately.

MAKES 6 SERVINGS.

Buttered Cabbage Wedges

1 head cabbage
  (about 2 lb)
1 teaspoon salt

¼ cup butter or
  margarine
Freshly ground black
  pepper

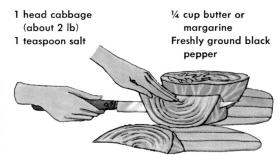

1. Discard outer leaves from cabbage; wash the head. Then cut cabbage into 6 wedges.

2. Pour water to ⅛-inch depth into large skillet; bring to boiling. Add salt, then cabbage. Simmer, covered, 8 minutes;

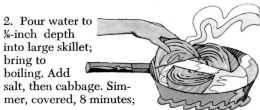

turn with tongs; simmer 7 or 8 minutes.

3. Pour off water. Return skillet to low heat until moisture has evaporated. Add butter; stir till it is melted and cabbage is coated. Sprinkle with pepper before serving.

MAKES 6 SERVINGS.

Mustard Sauce

2 tablespoons butter
  or margarine
2 tablespoons flour
½ teaspoon salt
⅛ teaspoon pepper
1 cup milk

¼ cup prepared
  mustard
1 tablespoon sugar
1 tablespoon cider
  vinegar
1 teaspoon Worcester-
  shire sauce

1. Melt butter in small saucepan; remove from heat. Stir in flour, salt, and pepper until smooth. Stir in milk. Bring to boiling over medium heat, stirring, until thick.

2. Gradually stir in mustard, sugar, vinegar, Worcestershire. Reduce heat, and simmer the mixture, stirring, 2 minutes. Serve warm.

MAKES ABOUT 1¼ CUPS.

An Italian Dinner

❁ ❁ ❁

Although this elegant menu is not planned for a large number of guests, it is without doubt company fare. It can easily be expanded to serve ten or twelve simply by doubling the recipes. The dessert recipes, however, do not have to be doubled—they will be adequate as is.

Place the first course, the melon or the baked clams, at each place setting before the guests sit down at the table. If you are having only six for dinner, the veal on a heated serving platter and the noodles pesto in a lovely casserole dish (preheated, of course) can both be served family-style by the host. The artichokes are placed on individual salad plates, each with a small cup of lemon sauce.

For a larger party, serve buffet-style, with the veal and noodles in separate chafing dishes or in electrically heated casseroles. A lovely platter of artichokes will enhance the buffet table while the sauce is set on the dining table to be served individually.

The ice cream bombe with flaming cherries jubilee will look quite spectacular and is a perfect finale to the meal. The equally delicious biscuit tortoni may be easier to prepare and serve if you are having many guests.

AN ITALIAN DINNER
(Planned for Six)

Melon with Port
OR
Baked Clams Oregano

Veal Scallopini
Noodles with Pesto Sauce
Artichokes with Lemon Sauce

Salt Crescent Rolls   Butter

Biscuit Tortoni
OR
Ice-Cream Bombe Jubilee, page 53

White Wine   Coffee

Melon with Port

1 large ripe honeydew or cantaloupe melon	½ cup port wine

1. Cut melon into six wedges. Remove seeds.
2. With melonball cutter, scoop a ball from center of each wedge. Fill hole in each with port. Refrigerate until serving time—several hours.
3. To serve, place each wedge on a serving plate with a galax leaf.

MAKES 6 SERVINGS.

Baked Clams Oregano

2 dozen clams in shells, well scrubbed	2 tablespoons grated Parmesan cheese
¾ cup butter or margarine, melted	4 teaspoons lemon juice
1 cup packaged dry bread crumbs	1 teaspoon dried oregano leaves
2 cloves garlic, crushed	⅛ teaspoon Tabasco
2 tablespoons chopped parsley	Rock salt
	Lemon wedges
	Parsley sprigs

1. In large kettle, bring ½ inch water to boiling. Add clams; simmer, covered, until clams open—6 to 10 minutes.
2. Meanwhile, in medium bowl, combine butter with bread crumbs, garlic, chopped parsley, Parmesan, lemon juice, oregano, and Tabasco.
3. Remove the clams from kettle; discard top shells. Remove clams from bottom shells; chop coarsely, and add to crumb mixture. Spoon into bottom shells.
4. Place a layer of rock salt, ½ inch deep, in a large roasting pan or two shallow casseroles; sprinkle with water to dampen.
5. Arrange filled clam shells on salt. Run under broiler just until golden-brown—about 5 minutes. Garnish with lemon wedges and parsley sprigs. Serve at once.

MAKES 6 SERVINGS.

Artichokes with Lemon Sauce

¼ cup olive or salad oil	1 teaspoon salt
6 lemon slices	⅛ teaspoon pepper
2 bay leaves	6 medium artichokes (about 4 lb)
1 clove garlic, split	

Lemon Sauce:

⅓ cup melted butter	3 tablespoons lemon juice
3 tablespoons olive oil	

1. In large kettle, combine 3 quarts water with ¼ cup olive oil, lemon slices, bay leaves, garlic, salt, and pepper; bring to boiling.
2. Meanwhile, trim stalk from base of artichokes; cut a 1-inch slice from tops. Remove discolored leaves; snip off spike ends.
3. Wash the artichokes in cold water; drain.
4. Add to boiling mixture. Reduce heat; simmer, covered, 40 to 45 minutes, or until artichoke bases feel soft. Drain artichokes well.
5. Meanwhile, make Lemon Sauce: In a small bowl, mix the butter, 3 tablespoons olive oil, and the lemon juice until well combined.
6. To serve: Place artichoke and small cup of sauce on individual plates. To eat, pull out leaves, one at a time, and dip in sauce. Discard prickly choke.

MAKES 6 SERVINGS.

Salt Crescent Rolls

2 pkg (8-oz size) refrigerated crescent dinner rolls	1 egg, slightly beaten
	2 teaspoons coarse salt

1. Preheat oven to 375F.
2. Shape crescents, and place on cookie sheet, as package label directs.
3. Brush crescents with egg; sprinkle with salt.

4. Bake 12 minutes, or until golden-brown.
MAKES 16.

Biscuit Tortoni

3 egg whites	Almond extract
¾ cup sugar	1½ cups heavy cream
Dash salt	¾ teaspoon vanilla extract
¼ cup whole blanched almonds	12 candied cherries

1. In small bowl of electric mixer, let egg whites warm to room temperature—about 1 hour.
2. Combine ¼ cup water with the sugar in a 1-quart saucepan; cook over low heat, stirring, until sugar is dissolved.
3. Bring to boiling over medium heat; boil, uncovered and without stirring, to 236F on candy thermometer, or until syrup spins a 2-inch thread when dropped from a spoon.
4. Meanwhile, at high speed, beat egg whites with salt just until stiff peaks form when beater is slowly raised.
5. Pour hot syrup in thin stream over egg whites, beating constantly until mixture forms very stiff peaks when beater in raised. Refrigerate, covered, 30 minutes.
6. Meanwhile, preheat oven to 350F. Place almonds in shallow pan, and bake just until toasted—8 to 10 minutes. Finely grind almonds in a blender.
7. Turn into a small bowl. Blend in 1½ teaspoons almond extract. Set aside.
8. In medium bowl, beat cream with ¼ teaspoon almond extract and the vanilla until stiff. With wire whisk or rubber scraper, fold into egg-white mixture until thoroughly combined.
9. Spoon into 12 paper-lined 2½-inch muffin-pan cups. Sprinkle with almond mixture; top with a cherry.
10. Cover with foil; freeze until firm—several hours or overnight. Serve right from freezer. Any leftover tortoni will keep several weeks in freezer.

MAKES 12 SERVINGS.

VEAL SCALLOPINI

4 large tomatoes (about 2 lb)
¾ lb mushrooms
8 tablespoons
   butter or margarine
1 small onion,
   finely chopped
1 clove garlic, peeled
⅔ cup dry white wine
Salt
½ teaspoon dried
   tarragon leaves, crushed
12 thin veal scallops
   (1½ lb)*
⅛ teaspoon pepper
Grated Parmesan cheese

1. For sauce: Dip tomatoes in boiling water a minute or two, then in cold water; pull off skins.

2. Cut tomatoes in half crosswise; discard seeds and any juice. Coarsely chop firm flesh of tomatoes. Measure 3 cups, and set aside.

3. Gently wipe mushrooms with damp paper towel. Slice.

4. Heat 5 tablespoons butter in skillet with tight-fitting cover. Add mushrooms, and sauté until golden-brown—about 5 minutes.

5. Add onion and garlic clove; cook about 5 minutes, or until onion is golden-brown. Add tomato, wine, ¾ teaspoon salt, and the tarragon, stirring to mix well. Reduce heat; simmer, covered, and stirring occasionally, 30 minutes.

6. Meanwhile, wipe veal scallops with damp paper towels. Season with ½ teaspoon salt and pepper.

° Have veal sliced for scallopini and pounded to ⅛-inch thickness.

7. Heat 3 tablespoons butter in a medium skillet. Over medium heat, sauté scallops, a few at a time, until lightly browned on both sides—about 5 minutes. Turn once, using tongs. Keep warm.

8. Return veal to skillet. Remove garlic from sauce. Pour sauce over veal; simmer, covered, 5 minutes.

9. To serve: Arrange veal and sauce on heated platter. Serve with Noodles with Pesto Sauce. Pass grated Parmesan cheese.

MAKES 6 SERVINGS.

NOODLES WITH PESTO SAUCE

1 tablespoon salt
1 pkg (8 oz)
   medium noodles

Pesto Sauce:

3 tablespoons butter
   or margarine
1 tablespoon olive or salad oil
¼ teaspoon crushed garlic
3 tablespoons chopped parsley
1 teaspoon dried basil leaves
½ teaspoon dried
   marjoram leaves

1. In large kettle, bring 3 quarts water and the salt to a rapid boil. Add noodles. Return to boiling; cook, uncovered, and stirring occasionally, 7 to 10 minutes, or just until tender.

2. Meanwhile, make Pesto Sauce: Melt butter in small saucepan; remove from heat. Add remaining sauce ingredients; mix well.

3. Drain noodles; turn into heated serving dish. Add sauce; toss until noodles are evenly coated.

A Warm Weather Menu

While we especially recommend this menu for a dinner party in the summertime, it can be served any time of the year if you substitute the poached salmon with lemon butter for the cold glazed salmon with sauce verte. The menu is flexible in variety and quantity and can be prepared with a minimum of work and time.

The lime sherbet with strawberries, so cool and refreshing, is an excellent warm weather choice. If you decide on the lemon chiffon pie you may want to omit either the English muffins or the new potatoes.

Keep the color scheme of your table decor as cool as the menu. A green- and white-flowered print cloth on a small round table with a centerpiece of white flowers would look very pretty. Or use green linen mats on a glass-topped table, and white ironstone plates or some gay Italian pottery.

A WARM WEATHER MENU
(Planned for Four)

Cold Cucumber Soup

Poached Salmon with Lemon Butter
OR
Glazed Salmon with Sauce Verte
Parsleyed New Potatoes
Fresh Asparagus Mimosa

Toasted English Muffins

Lime Sherbert with Strawberries
OR
Lemon Chiffon Pie, page 64

White Wine   Iced Coffee

Cold Cucumber Soup

1½ cucumbers (about 1 lb)	¼ teaspoon salt
1½ tablespoons butter or	¾ cup chicken broth
margarine	½ cup milk
1 tablespoon flour	½ cup light cream

1. Pare cucumbers; cut in half lengthwise. With teaspoon, scoop out and discard seeds. Cut cucumber into ¼-inch pieces.

2. In large saucepan, sauté cucumber in hot butter 5 minutes, or until transparent. Remove from heat. Stir in flour and salt until blended. Gradually add chicken broth and milk.

3. Cook over medium heat, stirring constantly, until mixture boils. Reduce heat; simmer, covered, 15 minutes.

4. Turn into electric-blender container; blend, at high speed, 1 minute. (Or put mixture through a sieve, pressing cucumber through.) Turn into a bowl.

5. Stir in cream. Refrigerate, covered, until very well chilled—at least 4 hours.

6. Serve in bouillon cups. Garnish with a slice of cucumber, if you wish.

MAKES 4 OR 5 SERVINGS.

Parsleyed New Potatoes

2 lb small new potatoes	2 tablespoons chopped parsley
¼ teaspoon salt	
¼ cup butter or margarine, melted	

1. Scrub potatoes. Pare a narrow band of skin around center of each potato.

2. Cook in 2 inches salted boiling water, covered, 20 to 25 minutes. Drain. Add butter and parsley; toss until evenly coated.

MAKES 4 SERVINGS.

Fresh Asparagus Mimosa

2 lb asparagus	3 tablespoons butter or
¼ teaspoon salt	margarine, melted
1 hard-cooked egg	2 tablespoons lemon juice

1. Cut off tough ends of asparagus. Wash stalks well. With vegetable parer, scrape skin and scales from lower part of stalks.

2. In large skillet, add salt to 1½ inches water; bring to boiling. Add asparagus spears; boil vigorously, covered, 8 to 10 minutes.

3. Meanwhile, separate white and yolk of the hard-cooked egg. Chop white and yolk separately.

4. Drain asparagus well. Arrange on platter. Drizzle with butter. Sprinkle egg white over asparagus, then egg yolk. Just before serving, sprinkle with lemon juice.

MAKES 4 SERVINGS.

Lime Sherbet with Strawberries

1 env unflavored gelatine	½ cup lime juice
2 cups milk	¼ cup lemon juice
1⅓ cups sugar	2 tablespoons grated lemon
½ teaspoon salt	peel
2 cups light cream	Strawberries, washed and hulled

1. In small heavy saucepan, sprinkle gelatine over ½ cup milk to soften.

2. In medium bowl combine remaining milk, sugar, salt, and cream. Stir until sugar is dissolved. Stir in lime juice, lemon juice, and peel.

3. Heat gelatine mixture over low heat, stirring constantly until gelatine is dissolved. Remove from heat; slowly stir into mixture in bowl.

4. Turn into ice-cube tray; freeze until frozen 1 inch in from edge.

5. Turn into chilled bowl; with electric mixer or rotary beater beat mixture quickly until smooth but not melted. Return to ice-cube tray.

6. Freeze several hours or until firm.

7. To serve: Spoon into sherbet glasses; top with strawberries.

MAKES 6 SERVINGS.

POACHED SALMON WITH LEMON BUTTER

1 cup dry white wine	4 salmon steaks
1 small onion, sliced	(about 2 lb)
1 stalk celery, cut up	⅓ cup butter or
Parsley sprigs	margarine, melted
1 teaspoon salt	⅓ cup lemon juice
1 bay leaf	3 lemon slices

1. In large skillet, bring wine, 2 cups water, the onion, celery, 2 parsley springs, the salt, and bay leaf to boiling. Reduce heat; simmer, covered, 15 minutes.

2. Meanwhile, rinse salmon steaks in cold water; drain.

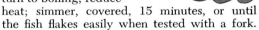

3. Add salmon to wine mixture, adding water, if needed, so liquid just covers salmon. Return to boiling; reduce heat; simmer, covered, 15 minutes, or until the fish flakes easily when tested with a fork.

4. Remove salmon from skillet with a wide, slotted spatula; drain. Place on heated serving platter.

5. Combine melted butter and lemon juice. Drizzle mixture over salmon steaks. Garnish salmon with parsley springs and lemon slices.

MAKES 4 SERVINGS.

GLAZED SALMON WITH SAUCE VERTE

4 salmon steaks	Chives
(about 2 lb)	Parsley sprigs
1 teaspoon unflavored	Lemon slices
gelatine	Cucumber slices
1 cup dry white wine	Sauce Verte,
Pitted ripe olives	far right

1. Cook salmon steaks as in the recipe above.

2. Drain steaks on wire rack. Carefully remove and discard skin. Place rack over a pan; cover steaks with plastic film. Refrigerate until they are very well chilled— several hours or overnight.

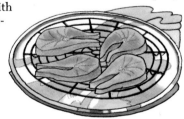

3. When ready to glaze salmon: Sprinkle gelatine over ½ cup wine in a small sauce-pan; heat, over medium heat, to dissolve. Stir in rest of wine.

4. Pour into small bowl set in a bowl of ice cubes. Let stand, stirring occasionally, till consistency of unbeaten egg white—about 10 minutes. Meanwhile, cut olives into strips.

5. Spoon most of thickened gelatine mixture over chilled salmon steaks until they are well coated. Decorate with olive strips and chives, as shown below.

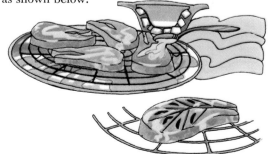

6. Spoon rest of gelatine mixture over the decorations, to hold them in place. Refrigerate at least 1 hour, or until the glaze is firm.

7. Carefully remove steaks from rack to chilled serving platter. Garnish with parsley sprigs, lemon slices, and thin cucumber slices. Pass the Sauce Verte.

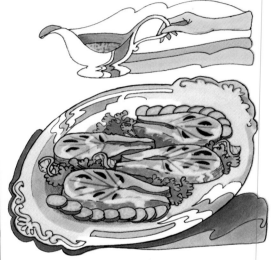

MAKES 4 SERVINGS.

Sauce Verte

1 cup mayonnaise or	2 tablespoons
cooked salad dressing	tarragon
⅓ cup chopped	vinegar
parsley	1 tablespoon
⅓ cup chopped	snipped dill
watercress	1 tablespoon
2 tablespoons capers,	snipped chives
drained	

1. Combine all ingredients in medium bowl or blender container. At high speed, beat with electric beater or blend till smooth.

2. Turn into a serving bowl or sauceboat. Refrigerate, covered, for 2 hours before serving.

MAKES ABOUT 1¼ CUPS.

A Festive Friday Night Dinner

This menu will certainly be appreciated by anyone who is fond of fish. It does, however, require some last-minute preparation, but the results will be well worth your efforts. Here is what you can do in advance:

Early in the day, wash and dry the bibb lettuce and store it in the refrigerator crisper. Make and refrigerate the dressing. Prepare the boula through step 2, ready for cooking. Prepare the baked tomato halves through step 4; and the herb rolls through step 4. Both will be ready for baking.

You may prepare the fillets of sole through step 7, and the apricot soufflé through step 3. The canned potato sticks need only to be heated.

If your dessert choice is the shortcake, prepare it ahead through step 5, ready for baking. Refrigerate the cake (no longer than three hours) and bake in time for it to be served warm. If the cake has been refrigerated for a couple of hours you will have to bake it a few minutes longer than the recipe indicates. For a pleasant change serve dessert and coffee buffet-style in the living room.

A FESTIVE FRIDAY NIGHT DINNER
(*Planned for Six*)

Boula

Fillets of Sole Florentine
Crisp Potato Sticks
Baked Tomato Halves

Bibb Lettuce
with
Oil and Vinegar Dressing
Toasted Herb Rolls

Warm Apricot Soufflé
with
Whipped Cream
OR
Old-fashioned Strawberry Shortcake, page 55

White Wine   Coffee

Boula

2 tablespoons butter or margarine	1 can (1 quart, 1 oz) green-turtle soup
½ cup finely chopped onion	½ cup light cream
2 pkg (10-oz size) frozen peas	½ cup dry sherry
1¼ teaspoons salt	

1. In hot butter in large kettle, sauté onion until soft—about 5 minutes. Add peas, salt, and ¼ cup water; bring to boiling. Reduce heat; simmer, covered, 10 minutes. Remove from heat; cool slightly.
2. Blend vegetable mixture, 1 cup at a time, in electric blender, covered, till smooth. Turn into bowl.
3. Return puréed mixture to the kettle. Add turtle soup, cream, and sherry; cook over low heat, stirring occasionally, until heated through.
4. To serve: Pour soup into a warm tureen or soup cups. Garnish each serving with a wheat cracker, topped with lightly salted whipped cream, if desired.
MAKES 6 SERVINGS.

Baked Tomato Halves

5 medium tomatoes	2 tablespoons finely chopped parsley
Prepared mustard	
Seasoned salt	Olive or salad oil
1 cup soft bread crumbs	

1. Preheat oven to 450F. Lightly grease a shallow baking pan.
2. Wash tomatoes; cut in half.
3. Arrange tomato halves, cut side up, in prepared pan. Spread lightly with mustard. Sprinkle with salt.
4. Combine bread crumbs and parsley; sprinkle over tomatoes. Drizzle a little olive oil over each.
5. Bake 10 to 15 minutes, or until bread-crumb mixture is golden.
MAKES 10 SERVINGS.

Oil and Vinegar Dressing

1 cup salad oil	½ teaspoon pepper
½ cup olive oil	½ teaspoon dry mustard
¼ cup dry white wine	½ teaspoon dried basil leaves
½ cup red-wine vinegar	½ cup chopped parsley
2 teaspoons salt	1 clove garlic, finely chopped

1. Combine all ingredients in medium bowl; beat, with rotary beater, until well blended.
2. Pour into jar with tight-fitting lid. Refrigerate at least 2 hours. Shake well just before serving.
MAKES 2½ CUPS.

Toasted Herb Rolls

1 loaf (1 lb) unsliced white bread	½ teaspoon dried thyme leaves
	½ teaspoon dried savory leaves
½ cup soft butter or margarine	1 tablespoon chopped parsley

1. Preheat oven to 400F.
2. With sharp knife, trim crusts from top and sides of loaf. Cut lengthwise down center, almost through to bottom of loaf, then cut crosswise at 1½ inch intervals. Place loaf on cookie sheet or in shallow pan.
3. Cream butter with thyme, savory, and parsley to mix thoroughly.
4. Spread top and sides of loaf with butter mixture.
5. Bake 15 to 18 minutes, until golden. Cut apart with scissors to serve. Serve warm.
MAKES 10 SERVINGS.

Warm Apricot Soufflé

4 egg whites (⅔ cup)	¼ teaspoon cream of tartar
¾ cup dried apricots	¼ teaspoon salt
1 tablespoon butter or margarine	¼ cup apricot preserves
Sugar	Sweetened whipped cream, chilled

1. In large bowl of electric mixer, let egg whites warm to room temperature—about 1 hour.
2. Meanwhile, in medium saucepan, combine dried apricots with ¾ cup cold water; bring to boiling. Remove from heat; let stand, covered, 5 minutes. Drain, reserving ⅓ cup liquid. Chop apricots very finely; add reserved liquid. Set aside.
3. Preheat oven to 350F. With butter, grease bottom and sides of a 1½-quart mold; sprinkle evenly with 2 tablespoons sugar.
4. Add cream of tartar and salt to egg whites; beat at high speed just until soft peaks form when beater is slowly raised.
5. Gradually add ⅓ cup sugar (about 2 tablespoons at a time), beating well after each addition. Continue beating until very stiff peaks form when beater is slowly raised.
6. With rubber scraper or wire whisk, using an under-and-over motion, gently fold apricot mixture into whites, just until combined.
7. Turn into prepared mold. Set in pan containing about 1 inch hot water. Bake 40 minutes, or until puffed and lightly browned.
8. Meanwhile, place preserves in small skillet; cook over low heat just until melted.
9. As soon as soufflé comes out of oven, loosen around edge of mold with small spatula; invert onto serving plate. Spoon preserves over top. Serve at once, with whipped cream.
MAKES 6 SERVINGS.

FILLETS OF SOLE FLORENTINE

2½ lb fillets
   of sole
¼ cup lemon juice
1 clove garlic,
   crushed
2 teaspoons dried
   tarragon leaves
1 teaspoon salt
1 cup Sauterne
2 pkg (10-oz size)
   frozen chopped
   spinach
⅓ cup heavy cream,
   whipped

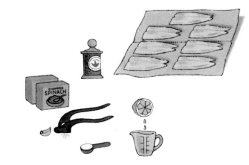

1. Make Hollandaise Sauce, at right.

2. Wash the fillets; dry well with paper towels. Brush both sides of the fillets with lemon juice.

3. Fold fillets into thirds, with dark side inside. Arrange them in a single layer in a large skillet.

4. Sprinkle the garlic, tarragon, and salt over the fillets. Then add the Sauterne; bring to boiling.

5. Reduce heat; simmer, covered, 10 to 15 minutes, or until fish flakes easily when tested with a fork.

6. Meanwhile, cook spinach as package label directs. Turn into a sieve; press against the sieve to remove any excess moisture. Return the spinach to the saucepan, and cover.

7. Remove fillets from cooking liquid; drain well. Strain liquid, and use to make Wine Sauce, at right.

8. Stir ⅓ cup hot wine sauce into spinach. Spread spinach evenly in 1½-quart shallow baking dish.

9. Arrange the fillets of sole in a single layer over the spinach.

10. Spoon the remaining wine sauce over the fillets and spinach, covering them completely.

11. Fold whipped cream into hollandaise sauce; then spoon this over the wine sauce.

12. Run under the broiler 2 to 3 minutes, until the top is golden.

MAKES 6 SERVINGS.

Hollandaise Sauce

1 envelope (1⅛ oz)
   hollandaise-
   sauce mix

Wine Sauce

2 tablespoons butter
2 tablespoons flour
1 cup strained
   cooking liquid
   from fish

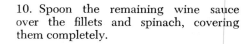

Make Hollandaise Sauce:

1. Prepare hollandaise-sauce mix as package label directs, using the ⅔ cup water specified.

2. Remove the hollandaise from heat, and set it aside to cool.

Make Wine Sauce:

In small saucepan, melt butter; remove from heat. Stir in flour; then gradually stir in cooking liquid from fish. Bring to boiling, stirring until thickened.

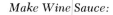

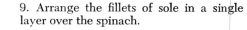

A Curry Supper

Although curry has become increasingly popular in this country, it is still considered exotic fare by many people. This menu is for guests with a taste for curry and for those who enjoy the adventure of trying something new and distinctive.

This is also an ideal menu for buffet service for a large number of people. If you are planning a buffet dinner you may wish to substitute a green salad for the braised spinach, since the salad will be easier to serve at the buffet table.

The puris, the fried bread puffs, will make a big hit with your guests. You may fry them ahead of time and reheat them in a low oven before serving. If you would prefer something simpler, serve English muffins instead.

A curry dish is at its best served with one or more accompaniments that complement the spicy curry sauce. Each of the accompaniments should be served separately in a small brass bowl on a brass tray or in small-size white soufflé dishes. To carry out the Indian motif, use a tablecloth or place mats of bright pink, the color so often seen in Indian saris. A large brass bowl filled with a variety of colorful fruits and vegetables makes a handsome centerpiece.

A CURRY SUPPER
(Planned for Six)

Avocado Soup
Toasted Crackers

Shrimp Curry
Fluffy White Rice
Braised Fresh Spinach
Curry Accompaniments
(Chutney, Chopped Green Pepper, Salted Peanuts,
Cucumber Slices, Diced Tomato, Sliced Banana,
Pineapple Chunks)

Puris—Fried Bread Puffs
OR
Toasted Buttered English Muffins

Honolulu Coconut Pie
OR
Lemon or Lime Tarts, page 67

White Wine   Coffee

Avocado Soup

3 ripe avocados (about 2 lb)	1 cup chicken broth
2 cans (13-oz size) vichyssoise	¼ cup lemon juice
2 cups light cream	½ avocado, for garnish

1. Peel 3 avocados. Slice 1½ into electric-blender container. Add 1 can vichyssoise, 1 cup cream, ½ cup chicken broth, and 2 tablespoons lemon juice.
2. Blend, at high speed, ½ to 1 minute, or until smooth. Pour into large bowl. Repeat. (Or press through a sieve into a large bowl; beat with electric mixer, at low speed, until smooth.)
3. Refrigerate soup, covered, until very well chilled—at least 4 hours.
4. Serve in a large glass bowl, decorated with avocado slices.

MAKES 6 SERVINGS.

Braised Fresh Spinach

3 lb spinach	¼ teaspoon salt
¼ cup butter or margarine	Dash pepper
1 small whole onion	1 tablespoon lemon juice

1. Wash spinach well; remove and discard stems; break large leaves. Pat dry between paper towels.
2. Melt butter in large saucepan or kettle over medium heat. Add onion. Add spinach, a handful at a time, tossing with butter until wilted.
3. When all is added, reduce heat; simmer 4 or 5 minutes, stirring occasionally, or until the liquid has evaporated.
4. Remove from heat. Add salt, pepper, and lemon juice. Turn into heated serving dish. Remove and discard onion.

MAKES 6 SERVINGS.

Puris—Fried Bread Puffs

2 cups sifted all-purpose flour	Salad oil or shortening
1 teaspoon salt	
¼ cup butter or margarine, melted	

1. Into medium bowl, sift flour with salt. Add butter; with fork, mix well (mixture will be crumbly).
2. Stir in enough water to make a soft dough—about 6 tablespoons.
3. Turn out dough onto a lightly floured surface; knead 5 minutes, or until dough is shiny.
4. Roll out dough very thinly, until you can almost see through it. Cut into 5-inch rounds.
5. Meanwhile, in electric skillet, deep-fat fryer, or saucepan, slowly heat salad oil (at least 2 inches deep) to 370F on deep-frying thermometer.
6. Gently drop dough rounds, a few at a time, into hot oil. Fry until they puff and are golden-brown—2 to 3 minutes. Turn with slotted utensil; fry 2 to 3 minutes longer.
7. With slotted utensil, lift out of oil, and place on paper towels to drain. Serve hot.

MAKES ABOUT 16.

Honolulu Coconut Pie

Filling

¾ cup granulated sugar	3 egg yolks
3 tablespoons cornstarch	¾ teaspoon vanilla extract
Dash salt	¼ teaspoon almond extract
2 cups milk	

9-inch baked pie shell

1 cup heavy cream	2 cans (3½-oz size) flaked
2 tablespoons confectioners' sugar	coconut, or 2 cups grated fresh coconut

1. Make Filling: In top of double boiler, combine granulated sugar, cornstarch, and salt. Gradually stir in milk until smooth.

2. Cook over boiling water, stirring constantly, until mixture thickens. Cover, and cook 15 minutes, stirring several times.
3. In small bowl, beat egg yolks slightly. Stir ½ cup hot cornstarch mixture into egg yolks, mixing well. Pour back into top of double boiler; cook mixture 2 minutes longer, stirring constantly. Remove from heat.
4. Stir in extracts; turn into small bowl; cover. Cool to room temperature—about 1 hour.
5. Refrigerate until well chilled—at least 1 hour.
6. Meanwhile, make, bake, and cool pie shell. Also, whip cream with confectioners' sugar until stiff. Refrigerate, covered.
7. To assemble pie: Turn filling into pie shell. Sprinkle with half the coconut. Cover with whipped cream. Sprinkle remaining coconut over top. Serve at once, or refrigerate no longer than 1 hour.

MAKES 8 SERVINGS.

SHRIMP CURRY

Curry Sauce

3 tablespoons butter or
   margarine
1 cup chopped onion
1 cup chopped pared apple
1 clove garlic, crushed
2 to 3 teaspoons curry
   powder
¼ cup unsifted
   all-purpose flour
1 teaspoon salt
¼ teaspoon ground ginger
¼ teaspoon ground cardamom
¼ teaspoon pepper
2 cans (10½-oz size)
   condensed chicken broth,
   undiluted
2 tablespoons lime juice
2 teaspoons grated
   lime peel

2 lb raw shrimp,
   shelled and deveined
   (18 to 20 per pound)
1 tablespoon salt
1 small onion, peeled and
   sliced
½ lemon, sliced
5 whole black peppers
¼ cup chopped chutney

1. Make Curry Sauce: In hot butter in large skillet, sauté chopped onion, chopped apple, garlic, and curry powder until the onion is tender—will take about 5 minutes.

2. Remove from heat; blend in flour, 1 teaspoon salt, the ground ginger, cardamom, and pepper.

3. Gradually stir in chicken broth, lime juice, and grated lime peel.

4. Bring to boiling, stirring constantly. Reduce heat, and simmer sauce, uncovered, 20 minutes, stirring it occasionally.

5. Meanwhile, cook shrimp: Rinse shrimp under cold running water.

6. In a large saucepan, combine 1 quart

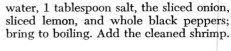
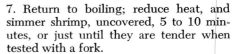
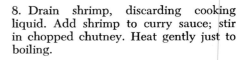
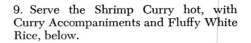

water, 1 tablespoon salt, the sliced onion, sliced lemon, and whole black peppers; bring to boiling. Add the cleaned shrimp.

7. Return to boiling; reduce heat, and simmer shrimp, uncovered, 5 to 10 minutes, or just until they are tender when tested with a fork.

8. Drain shrimp, discarding cooking liquid. Add shrimp to curry sauce; stir in chopped chutney. Heat gently just to boiling.

9. Serve the Shrimp Curry hot, with Curry Accompaniments and Fluffy White Rice, below.

MAKES 6 SERVINGS.

CURRY ACCOMPANIMENTS

Chutney
Pickled watermelon rind
Chopped green pepper
Chopped green onion
Diced avocado
Cucumber slices
Diced tomato
Salted nuts; peanuts
Sliced banana; raisins
Pineapple chunks

FLUFFY WHITE RICE

1½ cups raw regular white rice
1½ teaspoons salt
1½ tablespoons butter or
margarine

1. In heavy, medium saucepan, with tight-fitting cover, combine 3 cups cold water with the rice, salt, and butter. Bring rice mixture to boiling, uncovered.

2. Reduce heat, and simmer, covered, 12 to 14 minutes, or until rice is tender and water is absorbed.

3. Fluff up rice with a fork.

MAKES 6 SERVINGS.

On the Terrace

❈ ❈ ❈

This tempting warm weather menu is appropriate for serving indoors or outdoors, depending on the weather and your serving facilities. What could be more refreshing on a hot summer night than chilled gazpacho soup? The main course, the lobster termidor, is light and delicious, too, as are the salad and the dessert selections.

To prepare the menu earlier in the day, make the gazpacho through step 5; the salad through step 3; and the bread through step 2. The lobster thermidor may be prepared through step 8 and refrigerated. At serving time fill the shells with the lobster mixture and bake as directed. Only the rice and the green beans must be cooked at the last minute.

The raspberry chantilly shortcake is so good that you will be delighted to have more servings than you need for your guests. The next day garnish the remaining servings with the fruit and whipped cream and enjoy it all over again.

A pastel-colored tablecloth and matching napkins are perfect in the summer months, and a natural straw basket filled with white or yellow daisies makes a charming centerpiece. If you are serving outdoors, yellow candles in hurricane lamps would be appropriate.

ON THE TERRACE
(Planned for Four)

Gazpacho

Lobster Thermidor
French-style Green Beans
Fluffy White Rice

Marinated-Mushroom Salad
Herb Bread

Raspberry Chantilly Shortcake
OR
Lemon Meringue Pie, page 63

Chablis   *Coffee*

Gazpacho

2 large tomatoes (1¾ lb), peeled	⅓ cup olive or salad oil
1 large cucumber, pared and halved	⅓ cup red-wine vinegar
1 medium onion, peeled and halved	⅛ teaspoon Tabasco
	1½ teaspoons salt
1 medium green pepper, quartered and seeded	Dash coarsely ground black pepper
1 pimiento, drained	2 cloves garlic, split
2 cans (12-oz size) tomato juice	½ cup packaged croutons
	¼ cup chopped chives

1. In electric blender, combine one tomato, half the cucumber, half the onion, a green-pepper quarter, the pimiento, and ½ cup tomato juice. Blend, covered and at high speed, 30 seconds, to purée the vegetables.
2. In a large bowl, mix the puréed vegetables with remaining tomato juice, ¼ cup olive oil, the vinegar, Tabasco, salt, and black pepper.
3. Refrigerate mixture, covered, until it is well chilled—at least 2 hours. Also refrigerate 6 serving bowls.
4. Meanwhile, rub inside of small skillet with garlic; reserve garlic. Add rest of oil; heat. Sauté the croutons in oil until browned. Set aside until serving time.
5. Chop separately remaining tomato, cucumber, onion, and green pepper. Place each of these and the croutons in separate bowls. Serve as accompaniments.
6. Just before serving time, crush reserved garlic. Add to chilled soup, mixing well. Sprinkle with chopped chives. Serve gazpacho in the chilled bowls.
MAKES 4 TO 6 SERVINGS.

Fluffy White Rice

1½ cups raw regular white rice	1½ tablespoons butter or margarine
1½ teaspoons salt	

1. In heavy, medium saucepan, with tight-fitting cover, combine 3 cups cold water with the rice, salt, and butter. Bring rice mixture to boiling, uncovered.
2. Reduce heat, and simmer, covered, 12 to 14 minutes, or until rice is tender and water is absorbed.
3. Fluff up rice with a fork.
MAKES 4 SERVINGS.

Marinated-Mushroom Salad

20 small whole mushroom caps

Marinade

½ cup salad oil	2 cloves garlic, crushed
½ cup cider vinegar	½ teaspoon salt
2 tablespoons finely chopped onion	½ teaspoon sugar
2 tablespoons finely chopped parsley	

Boston-lettuce leaves
Watercress sprigs

1. Wash mushroom caps well. Dry on paper towels.
2. In medium bowl, combine all ingredients for marinade. Toss mushroom caps with marinade, coating well.
3. Refrigerate, covered, at least 1½ hours.
4. To serve: Arrange lettuce and watercress on 4 salad plates. With slotted spoon, remove mushroom caps from marinade. Place 5 on each salad plate. Pour over remaining marinade, if desired.
MAKES 4 SERVINGS.

Herb Bread

½ cup soft butter or margarine	¼ teaspoon pepper
2 tablespoons finely chopped parsley	1 loaf French bread, about 15 inches long
1 teaspoon dried thyme leaves	
1 teaspoon dried marjoram leaves	

1. In small bowl, combine butter, parsley, thyme, marjoram, and pepper; beat until well blended.
2. Slit bread in half lengthwise. Make diagonal cuts, at 1-inch intervals, in cut side of each half, being careful not to cut through bottom crust. Spread butter mixture over cut surfaces.
3. To serve: Preheat oven to 400F. Bake bread, wrapped in foil, 15 minutes, or until heated through.
MAKES 1 LOAF.

Raspberry Chantilly Shortcake
Meringue Cake

1 pkg yellow-cake mix	¼ teaspoon cream of tartar
2 eggs	½ cup sugar
2 egg whites	¼ teaspoon vanilla extract
Dash salt	

Raspberry Chantilly

1 pkg (10 oz) quick-thaw raspberries	1 teaspoon cornstarch
3 tablespoons sugar	1 cup heavy cream

1. Make Meringue Cake: Preheat oven to 350F. Grease and flour 1 (9-inch) layer-cake pan and 2 (8-inch) layer-cake pans.
2. Prepare cake mix, using 2 eggs and water, as package label directs. Pour half of batter into the 9-inch pan; divide other half evenly between the 8-inch pans.
3. Make meringue: In medium bowl, with electric mixer at medium speed, beat egg whites with salt and cream of tartar just until soft peaks form when beater is slowly raised.
4. Gradually add ½ cup sugar, 1 tablespoon at a time, beating well after each addition. Beat in vanilla; continue beating until stiff peaks form.
5. Divide meringue, and spread half evenly over batter in each 8-inch pan, covering batter completely.
6. Bake all layers 35 to 40 minutes, or until cake tester inserted in center comes out clean.
7. Let layers cool 5 minutes. Loosen around edges; turn out. Place 8-inch layers, meringue side up, on wire rack. Cool all completely. (Wrap 9-inch layer; freeze for another day.)
8. Make Raspberry Chantilly: Thaw raspberries; drain, reserving juice. Set aside 10 raspberries, for garnish.
9. In small saucepan, combine sugar and cornstarch until well mixed. Slowly stir in raspberry juice.
10. Cook over medium heat, stirring constantly, until mixture comes to boiling and thickens. Reduce heat; simmer 5 minutes.
11. Remove from heat. Stir in raspberries. Refrigerate until very well chilled.
12. Beat cream until stiff. Fold in chilled raspberry mixture.
13. Place one cake layer, meringue side up, on serving plate. Spread with half of raspberry chantilly. Top with other layer, meringue side up. Spread with remaining raspberry chantilly. Garnish with reserved raspberries. Refrigerate until well chilled.
MAKES 8 SERVINGS.

LOBSTER THERMIDOR

1 small onion, peeled
  and sliced
½ lemon, sliced
1 tablespoon salt
5 whole black peppers
1 bay leaf
5 (6-oz size) frozen
  rock-lobster tails
2 tablespoons sherry

Sauce

⅓ cup butter or
  margarine
¼ cup unsifted
  all-purpose flour
½ teaspoon salt
Dash mace
¼ teaspoon paprika
1½ cups light cream
1 tablespoon sherry
½ cup grated sharp
  Cheddar cheese

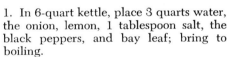

1. In 6-quart kettle, place 3 quarts water, the onion, lemon, 1 tablespoon salt, the black peppers, and bay leaf; bring to boiling.

2. Unwrap frozen lobster tails. With tongs, lower into boiling mixture; return to boiling. Reduce heat, and simmer the lobster tails, covered, 9 minutes.

3. With tongs or slotted spoon, remove lobster tails from kettle. Set aside until cool enough to handle. Discard the cooking liquid.

4. To remove meat from shells: With scissors, carefully cut away thin undershell, and discard. Then insert fingers between shell and meat, and gently pull out meat in one piece. Wash four shells; dry with paper towels, and set aside.

5. Cut lobster meat into bite-size pieces. Place in medium bowl; toss with 2 tablespoons sherry.

6. Preheat oven to 450F.

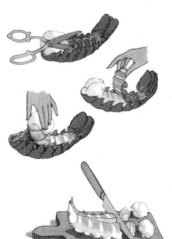

7. Make Sauce: Melt butter in 2-quart saucepan; remove from heat. Stir in flour, salt, mace, and paprika until smooth. Gradually stir in the light cream.

8. Bring to boiling, stirring constantly. Reduce heat, and simmer 2 to 3 minutes. Add the lobster meat and 1 tablespoon sherry; cook over low heat, stirring frequently, until lobster is heated through. Remove from heat.

9. Spoon into shells, mounding it high. Sprinkle with grated cheese and a little paprika, if desired. Place filled shells on cookie sheet. (Prop up tails with crushed aluminum foil, to keep them steady.)

10. Bake 10 to 12 minutes, or until cheese is melted and lightly browned. If desired, garnish with lemon wedges and watercress. Serve with French-Style Green Beans, below. MAKES 4 SERVINGS.

FRENCH-STYLE GREEN BEANS

1 lb fresh green beans
1 teaspoon salt
Boiling water
3 tablespoons butter or
  margarine

1. Wash beans under cold running water; drain.

2. With tip of paring knife, trim ends of beans. Then cut each in half lengthwise. (If beans are large and wide, cut in thirds.)

3. Place beans in 2½-quart saucepan. Add salt and boiling water to measure 1 inch.

4. Boil beans gently, covered, 12 to 15 minutes, or just until they are tender-crisp.

5. Drain beans, and toss with butter. MAKES 4 SERVINGS.

A French Dinner

❀ ❀ ❀

This distinctive menu is perfect for dinner by candlelight on Saturday night or for any gala occasion.

We assume that your guests enjoy French favorites and that they will relish the snails or the mussels. Of the two, the snails may be easier to prepare if you are pressed for time. Canned snails along with the shells in which to cook them can be purchased in most gourmet or specialty shops. Prepare them through step 4 and bake as directed at serving time. If you do not have escargot dishes, serve them in soup plates with small fish forks. The mussels may be prepared ahead through step 2. They will take 10 to 15 minutes to finish. Spoon the sauce over the mussels and serve them in soup plates with fish forks.

The coq au vin is prepared the day before and allowed to stand in the wine mixture to take on more flavor. On the day of the party you will only have to bake the chicken, potatoes, and onions until they are tender. Be sure to use an attractive casserole for the coq au vin so that it can be brought to the table in the baking dish. The petit pois can be cooking while the guests are eating the first course.

Both desserts are exceptionally good. The fruit is refreshing and will look very attractive served in the individual pineapple shells. The chocolate mousse pie is as delicious as it is easy to make. Decorate it with swirls of whipped cream put through a rosette tube in a pastry bag. Set the pie plate in a silver pie holder or in a pretty shallow dish to cover the pie plate. Serve small cups of strong coffee after the dessert.

A FRENCH DINNER
(Planned for Four)

Snails in Garlic Butter
OR
Moules Marinière

Coq au Vin
with
New Potatoes
Petits Pois

French Bread   Sweet Butter

Fresh Pineapple in Shell
OR
Chocolate Mousse Pie

Red Burgundy   Demitasse

Snails in Garlic Butter

1 can snails with shells (7½-oz can, 1½ dozen shells)	1 tablespoon lemon juice
½ cup soft butter or margarine	¾ teaspoon salt
2 or 3 cloves garlic, crushed	¾ teaspoon dried chervil leaves
1 shallot, finely chopped	⅛ teaspoon nutmeg
1½ tablespoons finely chopped parsley	

1. Prepare several hours before serving. Wash snail shells, and drain well on paper towels. Drain snails thoroughly; set aside.
2. In medium bowl, combine butter with remaining ingredients; mix well.
3. Place a little butter mixture—a generous ¼ teaspoon—in each shell. Push a drained snail into each shell; cover with more butter mixture.
4. Arrange filled shells carefully, open ends up, in a flat baking dish or special escargot (snail) dishes. Cover, and refrigerate.
5. To serve: Preheat oven to 400F. Bake snails in shells, uncovered, 8 to 10 minutes, or until butter mixture is very bubbly. Serve immediately.
MAKES 4 SERVINGS.

Moules Marinière

3 dozen mussels	½ cup chopped parsley
1½ cups chopped onion	⅛ teaspoon pepper
1 clove garlic, crushed	Pinch dried thyme leaves
⅓ cup butter or margarine	2 tablespoons soft butter or margarine
2 cups Chablis	
2 tablespoons lemon juice	1 teaspoon flour

1. Check mussels, discarding any that are not tightly closed. Scrub well under cold running water, to remove sand and seaweed. With a sharp knife, trim off the "beard" around edges. Place mussels in large bowl; cover with cold water. Let soak 1 to 2 hours.
2. Lift mussels from water, and place in a colander. Rinse with cold water; let drain.
3. In 6-quart kettle, sauté onion and garlic in ⅓ cup butter until golden and tender—about 10 minutes. Add wine, lemon juice, ¼ cup parsley, the pepper, and thyme; bring to boiling. Add mussels; cook over high heat, covered, 5 to 8 minutes, or until shells open. Shake kettle frequently, so mussels will cook uniformly.
4. With slotted utensil, remove mussels to heated serving dish. Cover with hot, damp cloth.
5. Quickly return cooking liquid to boiling; boil, uncovered, until reduced to about 2 cups—about 5 minutes. Mix soft butter with flour until smooth. Stir into boiling liquid, and cook, stirring, 2 minutes longer. Taste, and add salt if needed.
6. Spoon sauce over mussels; sprinkle with remaining parsley. Serve immediately.
MAKES 4 TO 6 SERVINGS.

Petits Pois

4 large lettuce leaves	Dash pepper
3 lb fresh young peas, shelled	2 tablespoons butter or margarine
1 teaspoon sugar	
½ teaspoon salt	

1. Line a medium-size, heavy skillet, with tight-fitting cover, with 3 large lettuce leaves.
2. Add peas. Sprinkle with sugar, salt and pepper. Dot with butter. Top with remaining lettuce leaf.
3. Cook over medium heat, tightly covered, 10 to 15 minutes, or until tender.
MAKES 4 SERVINGS.
NOTE: Or use 2 packages (10-oz size) frozen tiny peas. Cook 8 minutes, as directed above. Spread peas with a fork; cook 8 minutes longer, or just until peas are tender.
MAKES 6 SERVINGS.

Chocolae Mousse Pie

8- or 9-inch baked pie shell	2 tablespoons sugar
1 bar (½ lb) vanilla sweet chocolate, or 1⅓ cups semisweet-chocolate pieces	4 eggs, separated
	Whipped cream

1. Prepare and bake pie shell. Let cool.
2. In top of double boiler, combine chocolate, sugar, and ¼ cup water. Cook over hot, not boiling, water, stirring frequently, until chocolate is melted.
3. Remove from hot water; let cool slightly. Add egg yolks; stir until well combined.
4. Beat egg whites just until stiff. Fold into chocolate mixture until well combined. Turn into pie shell.
5. Refrigerate until well chilled—at least 6 hours. At serving time, decorate top with whipped cream.
MAKES 6 SERVINGS.

COQ AU VIN WITH NEW POTATOES

2½-lb broiler-
    fryer, quartered
6 bacon slices,
    diced
2 tablespoons
    butter or
    margarine
8 small white
    onions, peeled
8 small whole
    mushrooms
⅔ cup sliced
    green onions
1 clove garlic,
    crushed
2 tablespoons
    flour
1 teaspoon salt
⅛ teaspoon pepper
¼ teaspoon dried
    thyme leaves
2 cups Burgundy
1 cup canned
    chicken broth
8 small new potatoes,
    scrubbed
Chopped parsley

1. Day before, wash the chicken, and pat it dry with paper towels.

2. In a 3-quart Dutch oven, over medium heat, sauté the diced bacon until crisp. Remove bacon from the Dutch oven, and drain it on paper towels.

3. Add the butter to bacon drippings; heat. In hot fat, brown the chicken quarters well on all sides. Remove the chicken when it has browned; set aside.

4. Pour off all but 2 tablespoons fat from Dutch oven. Add the white onions, mushrooms, green onions, and garlic to the Dutch oven. Over low heat, cook, covered, and stirring occasionally, for 10 minutes.

5. Remove from heat; stir in the flour, salt, pepper, and thyme leaves. Gradually add the Burgundy and chicken broth; bring mixture to boiling, stirring.

6. Remove from heat. Add the potatoes, chicken, and bacon to Dutch oven; mix well. Cover, and refrigerate overnight.

7. The next day, about 2 hours before serving time, preheat oven to 400F.

8. Bake Coq au Vin, covered, about 1 hour and 50 minutes, or until the chicken and the potatoes are tender.

9. Sprinkle top with chopped parsley before serving. MAKES 4 SERVINGS.

FRESH PINEAPPLE IN SHELL

1 medium-size fresh,
    ripe pineapple
¼ cup Cointreau
2 tablespoons
    confectioners'
    sugar
1 cup fresh
    strawberries
1 cup seedless
    green grapes,
    halved

1. With a long-bladed, sharp knife, cut the pineapple, right through the frond, into quarters. With scissors, snip off the tips of the frond, if desired.

2. Remove pineapple, in one piece, from shells. Refrigerate the shells.

3. Cut core from pineapple, and discard. Cut pineapple into chunks; place chunks in a large bowl. Add the Cointreau and the confectioners' sugar; mix gently.

4. Refrigerate pineapple, covered, 3 hours, or until you are ready to serve.

5. Meanwhile, wash the strawberries; drain. Reserve a few berries for garnish. Hull remaining berries, and slice. Refrigerate all the berries until ready to use. Also refrigerate the green grapes.

6. Just before serving, toss sliced strawberries and halved green grapes with the pineapple chunks. Spoon fruit into chilled pineapple shells. Garnish with reserved whole strawberries. MAKES 4 SERVINGS.

A Backyard Supper

Dining outdoors has a universal appeal and is particularly popular in the summertime. This supper is the time when you can set your table with attractive paper plates, a colorful paper tablecloth and napkins, which are quite appropriate for this informal get-together. They make your cleaning-up chores easier too.

If a few more neighbors unexpectedly drop by, this menu, which serves four, can be expanded to serve eight by doubling the amounts of chicken and corn on the cob. The chicken may be served directly from the electric skillet in which it was cooked. If there is an electric outlet outdoors, it may be cooked right on the scene, at least during the last half hour.

In preparing the spinach salad, be certain to use young, tender spinach; any other kind will be too tough to eat raw.

Make the baking powder biscuits from a packaged biscuit mix as the label directs, or use the refrigerated ones, which require only last-minute baking.

The moist delicious applesauce cake or the unusual raisin pecan pie may not be completely eaten by your guests, but both will keep very well in the refrigerator.

A BACKYARD SUPPER
(Planned for Four)

Golden-Fried Chicken
Corn on the Cob
OR
Corn Pudding

Fresh-Spinach Salad
Hot Baking Powder Biscuits   Butter

Applesauce-Date Cake
with
Cream Cheese Frosting
OR
Aunt Lula's Pie

Iced Tea

Corn Pudding

2 pkg (10-oz size) frozen corn, thawed and drained
3 eggs, well beaten
¼ cup unsifted all-purpose flour
1 teaspoon salt
¼ teaspoon white pepper
1 tablespoon sugar
Dash nutmeg
2 tablespoons butter or margarine, melted
2 cups light cream

1. Preheat oven to 325F. Lightly grease a 1½-quart casserole.
2. In a large bowl, combine corn and eggs; mix well.
3. Combine flour, salt, pepper, sugar, and nutmeg. Stir into corn mixture.
4. Add butter and cream; mix well. Pour into prepared casserole. Set casserole in pan; pour hot water to 1-inch depth around casserole.
5. Bake, uncovered, 1 hour and 10 minutes, or until pudding is firm and knife inserted in center comes out clean. Serve hot.

MAKES 6 SERVINGS.

Fresh-Spinach Salad

Dressing

2 tablespoons white-wine vinegar
2 tablespoons lemon juice
½ cup salad oil
1 teaspoon salt
¼ teaspoon pepper
1 teaspoon sugar
½ teaspoon dry mustard
1 clove garlic (optional)

Salad

¾ lb tender young spinach
6 green onions, thinly sliced (¼ cup)
½ cup sliced radishes
1 small cucumber, pared and thinly sliced

1. Make Dressing: Combine all dressing ingredients in jar with tight-fitting lid; shake vigorously. Refrigerate until ready to use.
2. Make Salad: Wash spinach, and remove stems. Tear leaves in bite-size pieces into salad bowl.
3. Arrange the other vegetables in groups on spinach. Refrigerate, covered, about 2 hours.
4. To serve: Remove garlic from dressing, and shake vigorously. Pour dressing over salad; toss until spinach is well coated. Serve at once.

MAKES 4 TO 6 SERVINGS.

Applesauce-Date Cake

2 cups unsifted all-purpose flour
2 teaspoons baking soda
1 teaspoon cinnamon
½ teaspoon allspice
½ teaspoon nutmeg
¼ teaspoon cloves
¼ teaspoon salt
2 eggs
1 cup light-brown sugar, firmly packed
½ cup soft butter or margarine
2 cups hot applesauce
1 cup chopped dates
¾ cup coarsely chopped walnuts

Cream Cheese Frosting

1. Preheat oven to 350F. Grease well and flour a 9-by-9-by-2-inch baking pan.
2. Into large bowl of electric mixer, sift flour with baking soda, cinnamon, allspice, nutmeg, cloves, and salt. Then add the eggs, brown sugar, soft butter, and 1 cup hot applesauce; at low speed, beat just until the ingredients are combined.
3. At medium speed, beat 2 minutes longer, occasionally scraping the side of the bowl and guiding mixture into the beater with a rubber scraper.
4. Add remaining applesauce, dates, and walnuts; beat 1 minute. Pour batter into prepared pan.
5. Bake 50 minutes, or until cake tester inserted in center comes out clean. Let cool in pan 10 minutes. Remove from pan, and let cool on wire rack.
6. Frost top of cooled cake with Cream Cheese Frosting, above.

MAKES 9 SERVINGS.

Cream Cheese Frosting

1 pkg (3 oz) cream cheese, softened
1 tablespoon soft butter or margarine
1 teaspoon vanilla extract
2 cups sifted confectioners' sugar

1. In small bowl of electric mixer, combine cream cheese, butter, and vanilla; with mixer at low speed, beat until smooth and fluffy.
2. Gradually add confectioners' sugar; continue beating, at medium speed, until fluffy.

Aunt Lula's Pie

9-inch unbaked pie shell
4 eggs, separated
2 tablespoons butter, softened
1½ cups sugar
1 cup chopped pecans
½ cup dark raisins
1 tablespoon cider vinegar
1 teaspoon vanilla extract

1. Prepare pie shell. Refrigerate.
2. Preheat oven to 325F.
3. In medium bowl, with wooden spoon, slightly beat egg yolks. Beat in butter until blended. Add sugar; beat until light and fluffy.
4. Add pecans, raisins, vinegar, and vanilla; mix well.
5. In medium bowl, with rotary beater, beat egg whites just until foamy. Add to nut mixture; stir until well blended. Pour into pie shell.
6. Bake 50 minutes, or until filling is crusty and golden. Let cool on wire rack.

MAKES 6 TO 8 SERVINGS.

GOLDEN-FRIED CHICKEN

3- to 3½-lb broiler-fryer,
  cut up
⅓ cup all-purpose flour
1½ teaspoons salt
¼ teaspoon pepper
Salad oil or shortening
  (about 1¼ cups)

1. Wash chicken pieces under cold running water. Thoroughly dry with paper towels. Fold under wing tips.

2. In clean bag, combine flour, salt, and pepper. Add chicken to bag, a few pieces at a time, and shake to coat evenly with flour mixture.

3. In electric skillet, pour in salad oil, or melt shortening, to measure one fourth inch; heat at 375F. (Or slowly heat oil or shortening in large skillet with tight-fitting cover.)

4. Add chicken, a few pieces at a time, starting with meatiest pieces; brown on all sides, turning with tongs. Remove pieces as they are browned. It takes about 20 minutes to brown all the chicken.

5. Carefully pour off all but 2 tablespoons fat from skillet.

6. Using tongs, return chicken to skillet, placing pieces skin side down. Reduce temperature to 300F, or turn heat low. Cook, covered, 30 minutes. (If using

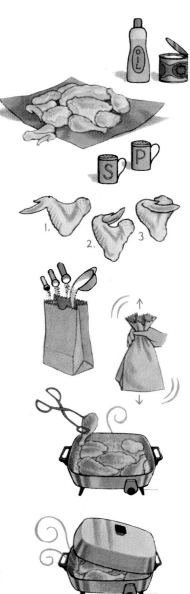

electric skillet, leave steam vent open.) Then turn chicken skin side up, and cook, uncovered, 10 minutes, or until meat is fork-tender and skin is crisp.

7. Remove chicken to heated platter, or place in napkin-lined basket. Serve at once.

MAKES 4 SERVINGS.

PICNIC CHICKEN

Prepare Golden-Fried Chicken. Remove from skillet; let cool about 10 minutes; then refrigerate, covered, until well chilled. Place individual servings in small plastic bags. Carry to picnic in a portable cooler or an insulated bag.

CORN ON THE COB

8 ears of corn
Butter or margarine, melted
Salt
Pepper

1. Cook corn as soon as possible after purchasing. (Keep refrigerated until cooking.)

2. In 6-quart kettle, start heating 4 quarts water.

3. Remove husks and silk from corn. Break off stem end of corn.

4. With tongs, slip ears of corn one by one into boiling water.

5. Cover kettle; return to boiling; boil gently 5 minutes.

6. With tongs, remove cooked corn from water to heated serving platter. Serve at once, with melted butter, salt, and pepper.

MAKES 4 SERVINGS.

A Late Supper

This menu is an excellent choice for supper after an evening at the theater or when you have finished playing a few rubbers of bridge. It would also be appropriate for Sunday night.

For these occasions the food does not have to be too substantial, but it should be interesting and delicious. Most important, you should be able to do most of your preparations earlier in the day so that the meal can be served with a minimum of last-minute work.

Here, for example, upon returning home the hostess can direct her attention to the food since she set her table before going out for the evening. The host serves the champagne or tends the bar.

The crêpes have been made ahead of time and left on cake racks to cool. The chicken filling, made in advance and stored in the refrigerator, is reheated over low heat. The crêpes are filled and baked as directed.

The jellied clam madrilène needs only to be cut into cubes and turned into sherbet glasses. The asparagus spears are arranged on lettuce on a large salad platter or on individual salad plates. The orange sherbet is unmolded and transferred to a serving platter. The cake is placed on a pretty cake stand and sprinkled with confectioners' sugar. Lastly, several kinds of refrigerated rolls are heated as the package label directs and put in the same oven with the crêpes.

Voilà! Thirty minutes after returning home, a delicious supper is ready to be served.

A LATE SUPPER
(*Planned for Six to Eight*)

Jellied Clam Madrilène

Chicken Crêpes

Green and White Asparagus Vinaigrette
Assorted Hot Rolls   Butter

Orange and Lemon Sherbert Orientale
with
Gold and White Angel Cake

Rosé Wine OR *Champagne*
Coffee

Jellied Clam Madrilène

2 env unflavored gelatine
1 can (16 oz) clam-tomato juice
1 can (12 oz) madrilène

¼ cup dry white wine
Lemon or lime wedges

1. In small saucepan, sprinkle gelatine over ½ cup clam-tomato juice, to soften—5 minutes. Heat over low heat, stirring constantly, until gelatine is dissolved.
2. Remove from heat. Add madrilène, wine, and remaining clam-tomato juice. Turn into a 13-by-9-by-2-inch baking pan or 3-quart shallow baking dish.
3. Refrigerate until firm—at least 2 hours.
4. At serving time, cut madrilène into about ½-inch cubes. Remove from pan with spatula, and place in bouillon cups or sherbet glasses. Garnish with lemon or lime wedges. Serve with crackers.
MAKES 6 SERVINGS.

Green and White Asparagus Vinaigrette

1 pkg (10-oz size) frozen jumbo green asparagus spears
¼ cup salad oil
¼ cup vinegar
1 teaspoon sugar
¼ teaspoon dried basil leaves
¼ teaspoon dry mustard

⅛ teaspoon salt
Dash pepper
1 can (15 oz) white asparagus spears, drained
½ can (7 oz) pitted ripe olives, drained
Crisp lettuce

1. Cook frozen asparagus as package label directs; drain well.
2. Combine salad oil, vinegar, sugar, basil, dry mustard, salt, and pepper in jar with tight-fitting lid; shake vigorously to blend.
3. In 13-by-9-by-2-inch glass baking dish, place cooked green asparagus, white asparagus, and olives. Add oil and vinegar mixture.
4. Refrigerate, covered, 4 to 6 hours. Carefully turn asparagus spears once or twice.
5. To serve: With slotted utensil, remove asparagus and olives from dressing; arrange on bed of lettuce.
MAKES 6 SERVINGS.

Orange and Lemon Sherbet Orientale

1 pint orange sherbet, slightly softened
1 pint lemon sherbet, slightly softened

¼ cup chopped preserved ginger in syrup

1. Spoon orange and lemon sherbets alternately into a large chilled bowl.
2. Sprinkle with ginger; swirl in gently.
3. Turn mixture into a 1-quart mold or serving bowl. Freeze until firm—several hours or overnight.
4. To unmold: Loosen around side with small spatula. Invert on serving plate; hold a hot, damp cloth over mold; shake to release sherbet. Repeat, if necessary. Or serve in bowl.
MAKES 6 SERVINGS.

Gold and White Angel Cake

1 pkg angel-food-cake mix
1 tablespoon grated lemon peel
1½ teaspoons lemon juice

10 drops yellow food color
2 drops red food color

Confectioners' sugar

1. Preheat oven to 375F.
2. Prepare cake mix as package label directs. Divide cake batter in half.
3. Fold lemon peel and juice and the food colors into half of batter just until combined.

4. Gently swirl white and yellow batters together, to marble. Turn into ungreased 10-inch tube pan. Smooth top of batter with rubber scraper, pressing the batter gently against side of pan.
5. Bake maximum length of time, and cool, as package label directs. Sprinkle top with confectioners' sugar before serving.
MAKES 12 SERVINGS.

CHICKEN CRÊPES

Crêpe Batter:

⅔ cup unsifted
    all-purpose flour
2 eggs
3 tablespoons cooled
    melted butter or mar-
    garine or salad oil
⅛ teaspoon salt
1 cup milk

Chicken Filling, at right
Sauce:

¼ cup unsifted
    all-purpose flour
⅔ cup sherry
1 can (10½ oz)
    condensed chicken
    broth, undiluted
2 cups light cream
½ teaspoon salt
⅛ teaspoon pepper
    Salad oil
½ cup grated natural Swiss cheese

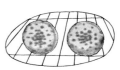

1. Make Crêpe Batter: In medium bowl, combine ⅔ cup flour, the eggs, 3 tablespoons butter, ⅛ teaspoon salt, and ½ cup milk. Beat with rotary beater until smooth. Beat in remaining milk until well blended.

2. Refrigerate the batter, covered, several hours or overnight.

3. About an hour before cooking crêpes, make Chicken Filling.

4. Next, make Sauce: In medium saucepan, blend flour with sherry. Stir in chicken broth, light cream, salt, and pepper.

5. Over medium heat, bring to boiling, stirring constantly. Reduce heat, and simmer, stirring once or twice, 2 minutes. Add half of sauce to chicken filling; stir until well blended. Set filling and rest of sauce aside.

6. To cook crêpes: Slowly heat a 7-inch skillet until a drop of water sizzles and rolls off.

7. Remove skillet from heat; brush lightly with salad oil. Pour in about 2 tablespoons batter, rotating pan quickly so batter will completely cover bottom of skillet.

8. Cook over medium heat until lightly browned; turn, and brown other side. Turn out onto wire rack. Repeat with remaining batter, to make 15 crêpes.

9. Preheat oven to 425F.

10. Place about ¼ cup filling on each crêpe; then roll up. Arrange, seam side down, in single layer in buttered 3-quart shallow baking dish. Pour rest of sauce over crêpes; sprinkle with grated cheese.

11. Bake for 15 minutes, or until the cheese is bubbly.

MAKES 6 TO 8 SERVINGS.

Chicken Filling

¼ cup butter or margarine
¾ lb mushrooms, chopped;
    or 1 can (6 oz) chopped mushrooms,
    drained
½ cup chopped green onion
2½ cups diced
    cooked chicken
½ cup sherry
½ teaspoon salt
Dash pepper

1. Heat butter in large skillet. Add mushrooms and onion; sauté until onion is golden-brown—about 10 minutes.

2. Add chicken, wine, salt, and pepper. Cook over high heat, stirring frequently, until no liquid remains in skillet. Remove from heat.

On a Hot Summer Day

Chicken salad may seem a rather mundane offering, unless it is as good as this one. Either one of our special desserts, the coffee-toffee pie or the fresh-fruit flan, makes this menu a happy choice when company comes.

It is also an ideal menu for warm weather dining since entertaining tends to be a bit more casual on sultry summer days. Most of the dishes may be made partially or entirely ahead. The chicken salad and the desserts, for example, can be prepared in the morning and chilled. The ingredients for the sangria, the avocado, and the corn sticks can be measured beforehand.

For a more substantial meal, you may serve the avocado as either the first course or the salad and offer in addition a hot vegetable, such as asparagus or broccoli with lemon butter.

A little advance planning will enable the hostess to remain cool and unharried, no matter how high the temperature soars.

ON A HOT SUMMER DAY
(*Planned for Six to Eight*)

Pitcher of Sangria

Chicken Salad
Avocado Halves

Corn Sticks   Butter

Blum's Coffee-Toffee Pie
OR
Fresh-Fruit Flan

Iced Tea

Sangria

1 bottle (1 pint, 7 oz) red Spanish wine	2 oz Cointreau
2 tablespoons sugar	2 oz Spanish brandy
1 lemon, sliced	1 bottle (12 oz) club soda, chilled
½ orange, sliced	24 ice cubes

1. In large pitcher, combine wine, sugar, and lemon and orange slices. Stir until sugar is dissolved. Stir in Cointreau, brandy, club soda, and ice cubes.
2. Let stand 15 to 20 minutes.
MAKES 6 TO 8 SERVINGS.

Avocado Halves

1 tablespoon finely chopped green onion	¼ cup cider vinegar
1 tablespoon finely chopped parsley	¼ teaspoon sugar
1 tablespoon finely chopped pimiento	¼ teaspoon salt
1 clove garlic, crushed	4 large ripe avocados (about 3 lb)
¼ cup salad oil	2 tablespoons lemon juice
	Salad greens

1. In jar with tight-fitting lid, combine all ingredients, except avocados, lemon juice, and salad greens; shake until well combined. Refrigerate at least 2 hours.
2. Just before serving, cut avocados in half lengthwise; remove pits. Sprinkle with lemon juice. Arrange on greens on individual salad plates. Shake dressing well; pour into avocados, filling the hollows.
MAKES 8 SERVINGS.

Corn Sticks

1¼ cups yellow cornmeal	½ teaspoon salt
⅔ cup unsifted all-purpose flour	1 egg
¼ cup sugar	1 cup milk
1 tablespoon baking powder	¼ cup salad oil

1. Preheat oven to 425F. Grease 2 corn-stick pans.
2. In medium bowl, stir cornmeal with flour, sugar, baking powder, and salt. Add egg, milk, and oil. With wire whisk or rotary beater, beat just until smooth—about 1 minute. Turn into prepared corn-stick pans.
3. Bake 12 to 15 minutes, or until golden-brown. Turn out of pans. Serve hot.
MAKES 14.
NOTE: Or use packaged frozen corn sticks, toasted in toaster.

Blum's Coffee-Toffee Pie

Pastry Shell

½ pkg piecrust mix	1 square unsweetened chocolate, grated
¼ cup light-brown sugar, firmly packed	1 teaspoon vanilla extract
¾ cup finely chopped walnuts	

Filling

½ cup soft butter or margarine	2 teaspoons instant coffee
¾ cup granulated sugar	2 eggs
1 square unsweetened chocolate, melted and cooled	

Topping

2 cups heavy cream
2 tablespoons instant coffee
½ cup confectioners' sugar
Chocolate curls

1. Preheat the oven to 375F.
2. Make Pastry Shell: In medium bowl, combine piecrust mix with brown sugar, walnuts, and grated chocolate. Add 1 tablespoon water and the vanilla; using fork, mix until well blended. Turn into well-greased 9-inch pie plate; press firmly against bottom and side of pie plate. Bake for 15 minutes. Cool pastry shell in pie plate on wire rack.

3. Meanwhile, make Filling: In small bowl, with electric mixer at medium speed, beat the butter until it is creamy.
4. Gradually add granulated sugar, beating until light. Blend in cool melted chocolate and 2 teaspoons instant coffee.
5. Add 1 egg; beat 5 minutes. Add remaining egg; beat 5 minutes longer.
6. Turn filling into baked pie shell. Refrigerate the pie, covered, overnight.
7. Next day, make Topping: In large bowl, combine cream with 2 tablespoons instant coffee and the confectioners' sugar. Refrigerate mixture, covered, 1 hour.
8. Beat cream mixture until stiff. Decorate pie with topping, using pastry bag with number-6 decorating tip, if desired. Garnish with chocolate curls. Refrigerate the pie at least 2 hours.
MAKES 8 SERVINGS.

Fresh-Fruit Flan

Flan Shell

¼ cup butter or regular margarine, softened	½ teaspoon grated lemon peel
3 tablespoons almond paste	1 egg white
2 tablespoons sugar	¾ cup sifted all-purpose flour

1 cup strawberries, washed and hulled
1 cup blueberries, washed
1 cup seedless green grapes, washed and stemmed
2 small ripe peaches, peeled and sliced
½ cup apricot preserves
1 tablespoon kirsch

Whipped cream

1. Make Flan Shell: Grease and lightly flour an 8-by-1½-inch round layer-cake pan.
2. In a medium bowl, with electric mixer at medium speed, beat butter with almond paste, sugar, and lemon peel until well combined.
3. Add egg white; beat at high speed until smooth. Gradually beat in flour until well blended. Turn into prepared pan; pat evenly over bottom and side. (If too soft to work with, refrigerate 10 minutes.) Refrigerate flan shell 1 hour or longer before baking.
4. Preheat oven to 300F. Bake shell 50 minutes, or until golden-brown. Let cool in pan on wire rack 15 minutes. Gently turn out onto rack, and let cool completely.
5. No more than 2 hours before serving: Mound strawberries in center of shell. Arrange blueberries, grapes, and peach slices around strawberries. (If standing longer than 2 hours before serving, fruit may make crust soggy.)
6. In small saucepan, heat apricot preserves over low heat just until melted. Stir in kirsch. Press through a sieve; spoon over fruit in shell. Refrigerate. Serve with whipped cream.
MAKES 8-INCH FLAN; 6 SERVINGS.

CHICKEN SALAD

5- to 5½-lb ready-to-
   cook roasting chicken
2 large carrots, pared and
   cut into 1-inch pieces
2 stalks celery,
   cut into 1-inch pieces
1 large onion, sliced
6 whole black peppers
2 teaspoons salt
1 bay leaf

1 cup mayonnaise or cooked
   salad dressing
2 tablespoons lemon juice
2 tablespoons milk or
   light cream
1½ teaspoons salt
Dash pepper
3 or 4 crisp large celery stalks
Crisp lettuce
Watercress
Tomato wedges

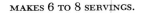

1. Remove giblets and neck from chicken. Then rinse chicken well under cold water. Place, breast side down, in an 8-quart kettle.

2. Add carrot, cut-up celery, onion, whole peppers, 2 teaspoons salt, the bay leaf, and 1 quart water.

3. Bring to boiling over high heat. Reduce heat, and simmer, covered, about 2 hours, or until chicken is tender. (After 1 hour, carefully turn chicken with wooden spoons.) Remove kettle from heat.

4. Let stand, uncovered, and frequently spooning broth in kettle over chicken, 1 hour, or until cool enough to handle. Lift out chicken. Strain broth, and refrigerate, covered, to use as desired.

5. Cut legs, thighs, and wings from chicken. Remove skin. Then remove meat from bones in as large pieces as possible. Set aside.

6. Pull skin from remaining chicken. With sharp knife, cut between the breastbone and meat, removing breast meat in large piece. Then check carefully, and

remove any additional meat. Refrigerate, covered, to chill—about 1½ hours.

7. Make salad: In large bowl, combine mayonnaise, lemon juice, milk, salt, pepper; stir until blended.

8. Cut celery, on the diagonal, into thin slices, to measure 2 cups. Add to dressing in bowl.

9. Cut large pieces of chicken meat into 1-inch pieces; there should be almost 5 cups. Add all meat to dressing. Toss lightly, to coat well.

10. Refrigerate, covered, until serving time—at least 1 hour.

11. To serve: Spoon salad into attractive bowl; garnish with lettuce, watercress, and tomato wedges.

MAKES 6 TO 8 SERVINGS.

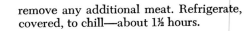

CHICKEN WALDORF SALAD

Chicken Salad, at left
2 cups coarsely diced
   red apple
¾ cup broken walnut meats

Prepare Chicken Salad, at left, reducing sliced celery to 1 cup. Add apple to dressing as soon as it is cut, to prevent darkening. Add walnuts, celery; toss lightly. Garnish with lettuce leaves and watercress. MAKES 8 SERVINGS.

CHICKEN FRUIT SALAD

Chicken Salad, at left
1 cup coarsely diced pared
   cucumber
1 can (13½ oz) frozen
   pineapple chunks, thawed
   and drained
¼ cup toasted slivered
   almonds (optional)

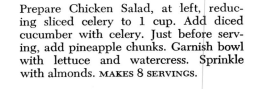

Prepare Chicken Salad, at left, reducing sliced celery to 1 cup. Add diced cucumber with celery. Just before serving, add pineapple chunks. Garnish bowl with lettuce and watercress. Sprinkle with almonds. MAKES 8 SERVINGS.

A Traditional Thanksgiving Dinner

For our Thanksgiving dinner the accent is on tradition with an innovation or two to please the younger members of the family.

The time-consuming preparations for a big holiday meal usually allow the hostess little opportunity to enjoy the day, her family, and guests. Our menu includes several dishes that can be made ahead and is designed to give the cook more leisure so that she, too, can participate in the festivities.

The hors d'oeuvres are prepared ahead of time and frozen, or they may be purchased ready to serve. If you are feeling very extravagant, serve caviar, either beluga or one of the less expensive varieties, with the cocktails. The canned lobster bisque needs only to be heated, with a little sherry, an exceptionally nice touch. The cranberry relish, the turkey dressing, and the desserts are all made the day before, which leaves only the turkey and the vegetables to prepare on Thanksgiving day.

Let autumn reign about the house and in your choice of table decor. You can select from the plentiful harvest of fall fruits and vegetables: yellow and green squash, pumpkins, gourds of all shapes and sizes, fall eggplant and cauliflower, green avocados, red and yellow apples, grapes of all colors, chestnuts, walnuts. An arrangement of autumn leaves or chrysanthemums would look quite lovely on the table, and, of course, an orange or gold tablecloth and napkins of both colors intermixed are the perfect colors for the season.

A TRADITIONAL THANKSGIVING DINNER
(Planned for Eight to Ten)

Hors d'Oeuvre
Chilled Caviar   White Toast Rounds
Triconas

Lobster Bisque with Sherry

Golden Roast Turkey
Old-fashioned Dressing   Giblet Gravy
Cranberry-Apple Relish
Butternut Squash OR Glazed Sweet Potatoes
Broccoli with Lemon Sauce

Grapefruit-and-Avocado Salad Platter
Assorted Hot Rolls   Butter

Old-fashioned Pumpkin Pie
OR
Hot Mince Pie with Rum Sauce, page 62
Ice Cream Turkeys

White   OR   Rosé Wine   Cider
Coffee   Liqueurs

Triconas (Hot Cheese Pastries)
Filling

2 pkg (8-oz size) cream cheese, softened
½ lb Greek cheese, crumbled
1 egg
3 tablespoons butter or margarine, melted

1 pkg (1 lb) prepared phyllo-pastry or strudel-pastry leaves
1 cup butter or margarine, melted

1. Make Filling: In small bowl of electric mixer, combine cream cheese, Greek cheese, egg, and 3 tablespoons butter; beat at medium speed until well blended and smooth.
2. Preheat oven to 350F.
3. Place 2 leaves of phyllo pastry on board; brush with melted butter. Cut lengthwise into strips about 2 inches wide.
4. Place 1 teaspoon filling at end of a strip. Fold over one corner to opposite side, to make a triangle. Continue folding, keeping triangle shape, to other end of strip. Arrange the filled triangle on an ungreased cookie sheet. Repeat with the remaining strips.
5. Repeat with other pastry leaves.
6. Bake 20 minutes, or until deep golden-brown. Serve hot.
MAKES ABOUT 7 DOZEN.
NOTE: If desired, make and bake ahead. Cool; then refrigerate, covered, overnight. Freeze half for another time. To serve: Arrange on cookie sheet; bake in 350F oven about 10 minutes, or until heated.

Cranberry-Apple Relish

2 large navel oranges
1 large red apple
1 lb fresh cranberries (4 cups)
1½ cups sugar

1. Grate peel of 1 orange into a large bowl. Remove peel and white pulp from both oranges.
2. Quarter and core unpeeled apple. Cut into ½-inch pieces. Wash and drain cranberries, removing any stems. Coarsely chop cranberries and oranges. Add fruits to grated peel.
3. Add sugar, stirring gently until dissolved. Refrigerate, covered, several hours or overnight.
MAKES ABOUT 5 CUPS.

Broccoli with Lemon Sauce

3 lb broccoli
Boiling water
Salt
2 eggs, separated
2 tablespoons heavy cream
2 tablespoons lemon juice
4 tablespoons butter or margarine

1. Trim broccoli; wash thoroughly. Split each stalk lengthwise into halves or quarters, depending on size.
2. Place broccoli in large saucepan. Add boiling water to almost cover; add 1 teaspoon salt. Cook, covered, 10 minutes, or until tender. Drain. Keep warm.
3. Meanwhile, in top of double boiler, beat egg yolks with cream and ¼ teaspoon salt until thickened and light colored. Gradually beat in juice.
4. Place over hot, not boiling, water; cook, beating constantly with wire whisk, until mixture thickens slightly. Remove double boiler from heat, but leave top over hot water.
5. Add butter, ½ tablespoon at a time, beating after each addition until butter is melted. Remove top from hot water.
6. In small bowl, beat egg whites until soft peaks form when beater is slowly raised. Fold into yolk mixture.
7. Arrange broccoli on heated serving platter. Top with sauce, and, if desired, garnish with lemon slices.
MAKES 8 SERVINGS.

Grapefruit-and-Avocado Salad Platter

2 heads Boston lettuce
1 small head romaine
2 ripe medium avocados, peeled and halved
2 large pink grapefruit, peeled and sectioned
1 cup thinly sliced celery
2 tablespoons snipped chives
Watercress sprigs
Special French Dressing

1. Wash salad greens; trim ends; discard with any discolored leaves. Crisp in crisper several hours.
2. In large bowl, place avocado halves and grapefruit sections, spooning grapefruit juice over avocado to prevent discoloration. Refrigerate, covered, until serving.
3. To serve: Arrange greens in shallow square serving dish. Slice each avocado half into 8 lengthwise slices. Reassemble halves, cut side down, and place one in each corner. Arrange grapefruit sections in center. Sprinkle celery and chives over all. Garnish with watercress. Refrigerate, covered, if not serving at once.
4. Let guests serve themselves to salad and Special French Dressing.
MAKES 10 SERVINGS.

Special French Dressing

1¼ cups salad or olive oil
⅓ cup cider vinegar
2 teaspoons salt
⅛ teaspoon pepper
¼ teaspoon paprika
Dash celery salt
1 teaspoon sugar
1½ teaspoons chili sauce
1½ teaspoons catsup
½ teaspoon prepared mustard
1 tablespoon lemon juice
1¼ teaspoons Worcestershire sauce
½ teaspoon prepared horseradish
Dash Tabasco
1 clove garlic, peeled

1. Combine all ingredients, except garlic, in a medium bowl. With wire whisk, beat until smooth and well blended.
2. Turn into a jar with a tight-fitting lid. Add garlic. Refrigerate several hours. Before serving, shake well; remove garlic. Refrigerate leftover dressing for later use.
MAKES 1⅔ CUPS.

Old-fashioned Pumpkin Pie

3 eggs
1 can (1 lb) pumpkin
½ cup light-brown sugar, packed
½ cup granulated sugar
1 teaspoon cinnamon
½ teaspoon ginger
¼ teaspoon nutmeg
⅛ teaspoon cloves
½ teaspoon salt
¾ cup milk
½ cup heavy cream
9-inch unbaked pie shell
Whipped-Cream Lattice

1. Preheat oven to 350F. In large bowl, beat eggs slightly. Add pumpkin, sugars, spices, salt; beat until well blended. Slowly add milk and cream.
2. Pour into shell; bake 60 to 70 minutes, or until knife inserted in center comes out clean. Cool on rack. Just before serving, decorate pie with Whipped-Cream Lattice.
MAKES 8 SERVINGS.

Whipped-Cream Lattice

½ cup heavy cream
1 tablespoon confectioners' sugar
¼ teaspoon vanilla extract

1. Whip cream with sugar and vanilla until stiff.
2. Using cream in pastry bag with number-3 (large rosette) decorating tip, pipe cream in lattice design over top of pumpkin pie.

GOLDEN ROAST TURKEY WITH OLD-FASHIONED DRESSING

Old-fashioned Dressing

12 cups fresh white-bread
    cubes
¾ cup finely chopped
    parsley
1 tablespoon poultry seasoning
1 tablespoon salt
1 teaspoon paprika
½ teaspoon pepper
½ cup butter or margarine
3 cups finely chopped celery
1 cup finely chopped onion

12-lb ready-to-cook turkey*
½ cup butter or margarine,
    melted
Giblet Gravy, at right

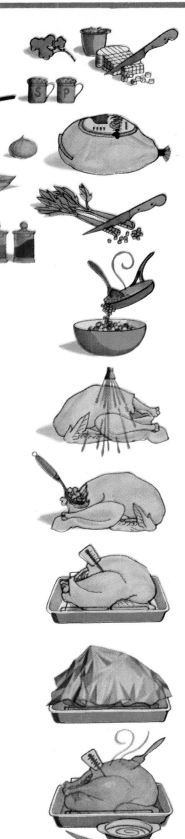

(Start roasting the turkey about 5 hours before serving time.)

1. Make Old-fashioned Dressing: In large bowl or kettle, combine bread, parsley, poultry seasoning, salt, paprika, and pepper; mix well.

2. In large skillet, melt ½ cup butter. Add celery and onion; sauté until golden-brown—5 to 7 minutes. Add to bread mixture; toss with wooden spoon until well blended.

3. Preheat oven to 325F.

4. Remove turkey giblets and neck; set aside for gravy. Wash and dry turkey very well inside and out.

5. Spoon dressing lightly into neck cavity. Bring skin of neck over back, and fasten with poultry pin.

6. Stuff body cavity lightly—do not pack, since stuffing will expand during cooking. (Spoon any remaining dressing into greased casserole; refrigerate. Bake, covered, with turkey during last hour of roasting.)

7. Tuck legs under band of skin at tail; if necessary, secure with poultry pin. Bend wing tips under body, or fasten to body with pins.

8. Place turkey, breast up, on rack in shallow roasting pan. Insert meat thermometer with bulb in center of inside thigh muscle or thickest part of breast muscle. (See note.)

9. Brush all over with some of butter. Place foil loosely over turkey. Do not tuck it around sides of pan.

10. Roast until meat thermometer reg-

* If using a frozen turkey, let it thaw completely as label directs—about 2 days in the refrigerator.

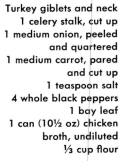

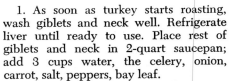

isters 170F—3½ to 4 hours. Carefully remove foil; cut skin to free legs. Brush turkey with more butter. Roast, basting every 15 minutes with any remaining butter and pan drippings, until thermometer registers 185F and bird is well browned—about 1 hour longer. Leg joint should move freely.

11. Place turkey on heated platter. Remove pins. Let stand 20 to 30 minutes before carving. Make gravy.

MAKES 12 SERVINGS.

NOTE: Since there are several breeds of turkey on the market, they vary greatly in shape and tenderness; this can make roasting time shorter or longer than time-tables indicate. To eliminate guesswork, use thermometer, and check label directions on turkey.

Giblet Gravy

Turkey giblets and neck
1 celery stalk, cut up
1 medium onion, peeled
    and quartered
1 medium carrot, pared
    and cut up
1 teaspoon salt
4 whole black peppers
1 bay leaf
1 can (10½ oz) chicken
    broth, undiluted
⅓ cup flour

1. As soon as turkey starts roasting, wash giblets and neck well. Refrigerate liver until ready to use. Place rest of giblets and neck in 2-quart saucepan; add 3 cups water, the celery, onion, carrot, salt, peppers, bay leaf.

2. Bring to boiling. Reduce heat; simmer, covered, 2½ hours, or until giblets are tender. Add liver; simmer 15 minutes. Discard neck. Chop giblets coarsely; set aside.

3. Strain cooking broth, pressing vegetables through sieve with broth. Measure broth; add enough canned broth to make 2½ cups; set aside.

4. Remove turkey to platter; pour drippings into 1-cup measure. Skim fat from surface, and discard. Return ⅓ cup drippings to roasting pan.

5. Stir in flour until smooth. Stir, over very low heat, to brown flour slightly. Remove from heat. Gradually stir in broth.

6. Bring to boiling, stirring. Reduce heat; simmer, stirring, 5 minutes, or until thickened and smooth. Add the chopped giblets; simmer 5 minutes.

MAKES ABOUT 3 CUPS

With a Holiday Air

This menu is a good choice for holiday entertaining, especially for the hostess who would like to serve something other than traditional dishes at Thanksgiving or Christmas.

Roast Cornish hen has an elegance appropriate for important entertaining. It is a glamourous main dish that is frequently found on restaurant menus, yet for some reason it is not often served at dinner parties. Perhaps hostesses hesitate to tackle it, fearing that it may be too difficult to prepare. Our recipe will dispel that myth and show you an easy way to make this impressive and delicious main course.

Of the two desserts, the pear tarte with whipped cream is a special favorite and the perfect ending for this meal.

WITH A HOLIDAY AIR
(Planned for Six)

Shrimp in Pink Mayonnaise

Roast Cornish Hens
with
Walnut Stuffing and Wine Sauce
Broccoli with Lemon Butter

Avocado and Endive Salad Bowl
Assorted Hot Rolls   Butter

Pear Tarte with Whipped Cream
OR
Ambrosia

Red   OR   White Wine   Coffee

Shrimp in Pink Mayonnaise

Sauce

1¼ cups mayonnaise or cooked salad dressing	2 tablespoons vinegar
⅓ cup chili sauce	1 teaspoon Worcestershire sauce
1 teaspoon grated onion	1 teaspoon prepared horseradish
1 tablespoon chopped parsley	
Dash cayenne pepper	

Shrimp

1 tablespoon salt	2 lb small raw shrimp, shelled and deveined
½ lemon, thinly sliced	
4 whole black peppers	8 lettuce cups

1. Make Sauce: In medium bowl, with rotary beater, beat mayonnaise with rest of sauce ingredients.
2. Refrigerate, covered, until used.
3. Prepare Shrimp: Bring 1 quart water to boiling in large saucepan. Add salt, lemon slices, black peppers, and shrimp.
4. Bring back to boiling; reduce heat; simmer, covered, 3 to 5 minutes, or until shrimp are tender.
5. Drain; discard whole peppers and lemon. Let shrimp cool. Refrigerate, covered, several hours or until well chilled.
6. To serve: Arrange a lettuce cup in each of 6 sherbet dishes. Divide shrimp into these. Spoon about 3 tablespoons sauce over each serving. Serve with lemon wedges, if desired.
MAKES 6 SERVINGS.

Broccoli with Lemon Butter

2 bunches broccoli (about 3 lb)*	½ cup butter or margarine
6 cups boiling water	3 tablespoons lemon juice
1 teaspoon salt	¼ teaspoon seasoned salt

1. Trim large leaves and tough portions from broccoli. Wash thoroughly; drain. Separate, splitting larger stalks in halves or quarters, depending on size.
2. Place in large saucepan or kettle; add boiling water and 1 teaspoon salt. Boil gently, covered, 10 minutes, or until tender. Drain well. Turn into serving dish.
3. In small saucepan, combine butter, lemon juice, and seasoned salt; heat until butter melts. Drizzle over broccoli.
MAKES 6 SERVINGS.
° Or use 2 packages (10-ounce size) frozen broccoli in butter sauce. Cook as label directs.

Avocado and Endive Salad Bowl

Dressing

6 tablespoons salad oil	½ teaspoon salt
2 tablespoons tarragon vinegar	1 clove garlic, split

1 small head Boston lettuce	1 tablespoon chopped chives
2 small heads Bibb lettuce	1 medium avocado
2 stalks Belgian endive	1 teaspoon dried dill weed
1 tablespoon chopped parsley	½ teaspoon dried thyme leaves

1. Make Dressing: In jar with tight-fitting lid, combine oil with vinegar, salt, and garlic; shake well. Refrigerate several hours.
2. Cut core from lettuce, and discard. Wash leaves; dry on paper towels. Tear in bite-size pieces into crisper. Slice endive, and add to lettuce; add parsley and chives. Refrigerate several hours.
3. To serve: Peel avocado; halve, and remove pit. Slice avocado lengthwise. In large salad bowl, toss crisped greens with avocado, dill, and thyme. Remove garlic from dressing; shake well. Pour over salad; toss until well coated. Serve at once.
MAKES 6 SERVINGS.

Pear Tarte with Whipped Cream

2 cans (1-lb, 14-oz size) pear halves	½ pkg (9½-oz size) piecrust mix
1 cup sugar	1 jar (9½ oz) marrons in syrup, drained (optional)
1 tablespoon butter or margarine	1 cup heavy cream, whipped and sweetened

1. Preheat oven to 450F.
2. Drain pears well. Cut each in half lengthwise; drain on paper towels.
3. To caramelize sugar: Cook sugar in large skillet, over medium heat and stirring occasionally, until sugar melts and becomes a light-brown syrup.
4. Immediately pour into bottom of an 8½-inch round baking dish. Arrange pears, rounded side down, spoke fashion, in caramelized sugar. Top with a second layer of pears, rounded side up, fitting pieces over bottom layer to fill open spaces.
5. Dot with butter. Bake, uncovered, 25 minutes, or just until caramelized sugar is melted.
6. Let stand in baking dish on wire rack until cooled to room temperature—about 1½ hours.
7. Meanwhile, prepare pastry, following package directions. On lightly floured surface, roll out to a 9-inch circle. Place on ungreased cookie sheet; prick with fork. Refrigerate 30 minutes.
8. Bake pastry at 450F for 10 minutes, or until golden-brown. Let stand on cookie sheet on wire rack until ready to use.
9. To serve: Place pastry circle over pears in baking dish. Top with serving plate; invert, and remove baking dish. Mound marrons in center. Serve with whipped cream.
MAKES 6 TO 8 SERVINGS.

Ambrosia

4 large oranges	4 medium bananas
1 can (13¼ oz) frozen pineapple chunks, thawed	4 tablespoons confectioners' sugar
2 tablespoons Cointreau, white rum, or orange juice	1 can (3½ oz) flaked coconut
	6 maraschino cherries

1. Peel oranges; remove white membrane. Cut oranges crosswise into ⅛-inch-thick slices.
2. Drain pineapple, saving syrup. Combine syrup and Cointreau; set aside.
3. Peel bananas. Cut on the diagonal into ⅛-inch-thick slices.
4. In attractive serving bowl, layer half the orange slices; sprinkle with 2 tablespoons sugar. Layer half the banana slices and half the pineapple; sprinkle with half the coconut.
5. Repeat layers of fruit and sugar. Pour syrup mixture over fruit. Sprinkle with remaining coconut.
6. Decorate with maraschino cherries. Refrigerate several hours, until well chilled.
MAKES 10 SERVINGS.

ROAST CORNISH HENS WITH WALNUT STUFFING AND WINE SAUCE

Stuffing

3 tablespoons bacon
   drippings
1 cup chopped onion
1 cup chopped green
   pepper
6 cooked bacon slices,
   crumbled
3 cups small dry
   white-bread cubes
1 cup coarsely chopped
   walnuts
1½ teaspoons salt
½ teaspoon dried
   thyme leaves
½ teaspoon rubbed
   sage

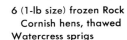

6 (1-lb size) frozen Rock
   Cornish hens, thawed
Watercress sprigs

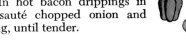

1. Make Stuffing: In hot bacon drippings in a medium skillet, sauté chopped onion and green pepper, stirring, until tender.

2. Add vegetables to rest of stuffing ingredients; toss lightly with fork, to mix. Use mixture to stuff hens. Close openings in hens with wooden picks; tie legs together.

3. Arrange hens, breast side up, in a shallow roasting pan without a rack.

4. Preheat oven to 400F. Make Basting Sauce, at right. Brush some over the hens.

5. Roast hens 1 hour, brushing occasionally with rest of sauce, until golden.

6. Discard string, wooden picks. Arrange hens on round platter; keep warm. Make Wine Sauce, right. Garnish hens with watercress. MAKES 6 SERVINGS.

Basting Sauce

½ cup butter or
   margarine
½ cup white wine
1 clove garlic,
   crushed
1½ teaspoons salt
½ teaspoon rubbed
   sage

Wine Sauce

3 tablespoons flour
1 cup white wine
1 cup currant jelly
1 teaspoon dry
   mustard
1 teaspoon salt

To make Basting Sauce (see the ingredients listed above):

1. Melt the ½ cup butter in a small skillet. Then remove the skillet from heat.

2. Add rest of basting sauce ingredients to butter in skillet, mixing well.

To make Wine Sauce (see the ingredients listed above):

1. Pour off drippings in roasting pan; return ⅔ cup drippings to pan. Gradually add the 3 tablespoons flour to the drippings, and stir to make the mixture smooth.

2. Add white wine, currant jelly, dry mustard, and salt. Bring mixture to boiling, stirring to loosen any brown bits in the roasting pan.

3. Reduce heat, and simmer the sauce, stirring occasionally, until it thickens. Pass wine sauce along with hens. The recipe makes about 2⅛ cups sauce—enough for 6 generous servings.

Dinner at Eight

This impressive menu, which features a classic entrée, duckling à l'orange, may seem rather elaborate for the beginner, but many of the dishes may be prepared the day before the party.

For example, all of the cocktail accompaniments—the herring in wine, the pâté maison, and the cheese ball—will taste even better if made the day before and refrigerated. The same thing holds true for the winter squash soup and the dessert.

Before the guests arrive, make the orange sauce for the duckling, prepare the stuffed mushrooms so that they are ready for baking, and place the salad greens in a bowl. Do not worry if the duckling must remain in the oven a little longer until the rest of the dinner is ready or until all of your guests have arrived. Duckling can hardly be overcooked.

If you do not have a set of the very pretty pots de crème pots, which are made especially for this dessert, use eight of the smallest size soufflé dishes or custard cups. To accompany the pots de crème, we suggest serving the large size, hard Italian macaroons, called amaretti, which come individually wrapped. Mound them in their papers in a beautiful compotier.

DINNER AT EIGHT
(Planned for Six to Eight)

Cocktails
Herring in Wine
Pâté Maison with Toast
Appetizer Cheese Ball   Crackers

Winter Squash Soup

Duckling à l'Orange
Wild and White Rice
Savory Stuffed Mushrooms

Green Salad with Endive
French Bread   Sweet Butter

Chocolate Pots de Crème, page 52
Almond Macaroons

Red Burgundy   Coffee

Herring in Wine

2 medium carrots, pared	12 pitted ripe olives, halved
3 jars (12-oz size) herring in wine sauce, undrained	¼ teaspoon whole black peppers

1. Cut carrots on the diagonal into ¼-inch-thick slices. Place in large bowl with rest of ingredients.
2. Refrigerate, covered, at least 24 hours before serving.
MAKES 12 SERVINGS.

Pâté Maison

½ cup sweet butter	1½ tablespoons cognac
1 large onion, sliced (1 cup)	½ teaspoon salt
1¼ lb chicken livers	Dash pepper
1 hard-cooked egg	Chopped green onion

1. In 2 tablespoons hot butter in skillet, sauté sliced onion until tender—about 10 minutes. Remove from skillet.
2. Heat remaining butter in same skillet. Add chicken livers, and sauté over medium heat 3 to 5 minutes, or until golden-brown. Liver should be pink inside.
3. Put half the sautéed onion, chicken livers, egg, and cognac in blender; blend at low speed just until smooth. Turn into bowl. Repeat with rest of onion, livers, egg, and cognac. Stir in salt and pepper. Turn into crock or small bowl.
4. Refrigerate, covered, until well chilled—overnight. Garnish with green onion.
MAKES 3 CUPS.

Appetizer Cheese Ball

4 pkg (3-oz size) cream cheese, softened	2 tablespoons grated onion
6 oz blue cheese, softened	1 teaspoon Worcestershire sauce
6 oz processed Cheddar-cheese spread	1 cup ground pecans
	½ cup finely chopped parsley
	Assorted crackers

1. In medium bowl, combine cheeses, onion, and Worcestershire. Beat until well blended.
2. Stir in ½ cup pecans and ¼ cup parsley. Shape into a ball. Wrap in waxed paper or plastic film, then in foil.
3. Refrigerate overnight.
4. About 1 hour before serving, roll cheese ball in remaining pecans and parsley. Place on serving plate, and surround with crackers.
MAKES ABOUT 30 APPETIZER SERVINGS.

Winter Squash Soup

1 butternut squash* (about 3 lb)	¼ teaspoon salt
2 cans (10½-oz size) condensed chicken broth, undiluted	Dash white pepper
	1 cup heavy cream
	¼ teaspoon nutmeg

1. Preheat oven to 400F. Bake whole squash about 1 hour, or until tender when pierced with a fork.
2. Let squash cool slightly. Cut in half lengthwise; discard seeds. With a spoon, scoop squash pulp from the skin.
3. In electric blender, combine half of squash pulp and 1 can broth; blend at low speed until well combined, then at high speed until smooth. Turn into bowl. Repeat with remaining squash and broth. Stir in salt and pepper.
4. Refrigerate soup, covered, overnight.
5. At serving time, heat squash mixture just to boiling. Gradually stir in ½ cup cream; cook slowly until heated through. Taste for seasoning, adding more salt and pepper if necessary.
6. Meanwhile, beat remaining cream just until stiff.
7. Serve soup very hot. Garnish each serving with a spoonful of whipped cream; sprinkle with nutmeg.
MAKES 6 TO 8 SERVINGS.
* Or use 3 packages (12-ounce size) frozen squash, partially thawed.

Savory Stuffed Mushrooms

12 to 16 fresh medium mushrooms	1½ cups fresh bread cubes (¼ inch)
½ cup butter or margarine	½ teaspoon salt
3 tablespoons finely chopped green pepper	⅛ teaspoon pepper
3 tablespoons finely chopped onion	Dash cayenne

1. Preheat oven to 350F.
2. Wipe mushrooms with damp cloth. Remove stems, and chop stems fine; set aside.
3. Heat 3 tablespoons butter in large skillet. Sauté mushroom caps only on bottom side 2 to 3 minutes; remove. Arrange, rounded side down, in shallow baking pan.
4. Heat rest of butter in same skillet. Sauté chopped stems, green pepper, and onion until tender—about 5 minutes.
5. Remove from heat. Stir in bread cubes and seasoning. Use to fill mushroom caps, mounding mixture high in center.
6. Bake 15 minutes.
MAKES 6 TO 8 SERVINGS.

Green Salad with Endive

1 medium head Boston lettuce	½ clove garlic
1 medium head Bibb lettuce	6 tablespoons olive or salad oil
½ small head romaine	3 tablespoons tarragon vinegar
2 Belgian endives	1 teaspoon salt
	Freshly ground black pepper

1. Prepare salad greens: Wash lettuce, romaine, and endive, and separate into leaves, discarding discolored or bruised leaves. Drain well, shaking in salad basket or placing on paper towels, to remove excess moisture.
2. Place cleaned greens in plastic bag, or wrap in plastic film. Refrigerate until crisp and cold—several hours. Also refrigerate salad bowl.
3. At serving time, rub inside of salad bowl with garlic; discard garlic. Tear greens in bite-size pieces into bowl; leave small leaves whole.
4. In jar with tight-fitting lid, combine oil, vinegar, salt, and dash pepper; shake until well combined.
5. Pour half of dressing over greens. With salad spoon and fork, toss greens until they are well coated and no dressing remains in bottom of bowl. Add more dressing, if desired.
MAKES 6 TO 8 SERVINGS.

DUCKLING À L'ORANGE

2 (5-lb size) ready-to-cook ducklings
2 teaspoons salt
2 cloves garlic, chopped
6 whole black peppers
4 unpeeled oranges, quartered
½ cup butter or margarine, melted
½ cup Burgundy
1 cup orange marmalade

Orange Sauce

2 pkg (6-oz size) long-grain-and-
 wild-rice mix
2 tablespoons butter or margarine

1. Preheat oven to 425F.

2. Remove giblets and neck from ducklings; set livers aside for Orange Sauce.
Wash ducklings well; drain, and dry with
paper towels.

3. Bring skin of neck over back; fasten
with poultry pin. Sprinkle inside of each
duckling with salt. Then stuff body cavity
with the garlic, black peppers, and orange
quarters.

4. Truss ducklings: Close body cavity
with poultry pins; lace with twine. Tie
the ends of the legs together, and bend
wing tips under the body.

5. Place ducklings, breast side up, on rack
in shallow roasting pan. Brush each duckling with about 2 tablespoons melted butter. Pour Burgundy over ducklings.

6. Roast, uncovered, 30 minutes. Reduce
oven temperature to 375F; roast 40 minutes. With baster, remove drippings from
pan as they accumulate.

7. Now, using spoons so skin will not
break, turn ducklings breast side down.
Brush with remaining butter; roast 20
minutes. Turn breast side up again, and
roast 30 minutes.

8. Spread ducklings with orange marmalade. Roast 10 minutes longer.

9. While the ducklings are roasting, make
Orange Sauce.

10. Prepare long-grain-and-wild-rice mix
as label directs, adding butter.

11. Remove poultry pins and twine from
ducklings. With long-handled fork or

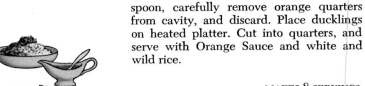

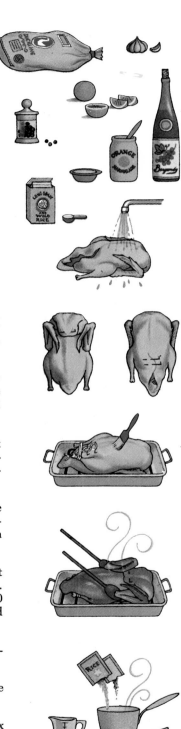

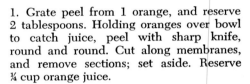

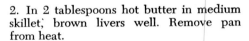

spoon, carefully remove orange quarters
from cavity, and discard. Place ducklings
on heated platter. Cut into quarters, and
serve with Orange Sauce and white and
wild rice.

MAKES 8 SERVINGS.

NOTE: If using frozen ducklings, let thaw
completely before stuffing.

Orange Sauce

4 large oranges
4 tablespoons butter
 or margarine
Livers from ducklings
4 tablespoons brandy
1 teaspoon minced garlic
3 tablespoons flour
3 teaspoons catsup
2 teaspoons meat-extract paste
⅛ teaspoon pepper
1½ cans (10½-oz size) condensed
 chicken broth, undiluted
½ cup Burgundy
⅓ cup orange marmalade

1. Grate peel from 1 orange, and reserve
2 tablespoons. Holding oranges over bowl
to catch juice, peel with sharp knife,
round and round. Cut along membranes,
and remove sections; set aside. Reserve
¼ cup orange juice.

2. In 2 tablespoons hot butter in medium
skillet, brown livers well. Remove pan
from heat.

3. Heat brandy slightly in small saucepan. Light with match; slowly pour over
the livers. When the flames subside, remove livers, and set aside.

4. Add remaining butter, reserved grated
peel, and garlic to skillet; sauté 3 minutes. Remove from heat.

5. Stir in flour, catsup, meat-extract paste,
and pepper until well blended. Gradually
stir in chicken broth, Burgundy, marmalade, and reserved juice.

6. Bring to boiling, stirring constantly.
Reduce heat, and simmer, stirring occasionally, 15 minutes.

7. Meanwhile, chop browned livers. Add
to sauce along with orange sections. Heat
gently.

MAKES 3 CUPS.

Saturday Night Buffet, Italian-style

We like this menu for an informal dinner to serve to guests with hearty appetites. It is one of our favorites, too, because there is little last-minute work for the hostess.

The antipasto platter, artfully arranged ahead of time and refrigerated until needed, can be served in the living room with the cocktails. Place the platter on a table where it is easily accessible, along with salad-size plates, forks, and cocktail napkins, and let it double as hors d'oeuvre and first course. You can also assemble an antipasto tray by using a variety of prepared foods, such as olives, anchovy fillets, marinated mushrooms, and marinated artichoke hearts, all of which are available in supermarkets.

The lasagna can be made ahead and arranged in a baking dish, which is also the serving dish, ready for the oven. (See note at the end of recipe.)

The salad greens, washed and dried in the morning, have been "crisping" in the crisper. Before your guests arrive, break the greens into bite-size pieces, toss together in the salad bowl, and store in the refrigerator. Use a bottled Italian-style dressing or an oil and vinegar dressing, which has been well chilled. Toss with the greens, a little at a time, coating but not "drowning" them, just before serving.

If you have a good Italian bakery in the neighborhood, you can offer several kinds of fresh, crisp Italian bread.

The dessert will look especially tempting if you place the fruit in a beautiful serving bowl and the cookies on a pretty cake stand. Offer a choice of café espresso and regular coffee. If you don't own an espresso maker, use the instant espresso coffee—it's quite good. Serve espresso with lemon peel, of course.

SATURDAY NIGHT BUFFET, ITALIAN-STYLE
(Planned for Eight)

Antipasto Platter
Roasted Peppers, Eggplant Appetizer
Pickled Garden Relish
Bread Sticks

Old-World Lasagna

Salad of Lettuce, Watercress, and Fennel
Italian Whole Wheat Bread   Butter

Peaches in Marsala
With Pine Nut Cookies

Red Chianti   Café Espresso

Roasted Peppers

8 medium sweet red peppers (2½ lb)	2 teaspoons salt
1 cup olive or salad oil	3 small cloves garlic
¼ cup lemon juice	3 anchovy fillets

1. Preheat the oven to 450F.
2. Wash red peppers, and drain them well.
3. Place peppers on cookie sheet; bake about 20 minutes, or until the skin of the peppers becomes blistered and charred. Turn the peppers every 5 minutes, with tongs.
4. Place hot peppers in a large kettle; cover kettle, and let peppers stand 15 minutes.
5. Peel off charred skin with sharp knife. Cut each pepper into fourths. Remove the ribs and seeds, and cut out any dark spots.
6. In large bowl, combine olive oil, lemon juice, salt, and garlic. Add the peppers, and toss lightly to coat with oil mixture.
7. Pack pepper mixture and anchovy fillets into a 1-quart jar; cap. Refrigerate several hours or overnight. Serve as an appetizer.

MAKES 1 QUART.

Eggplant Appetizer

1 large eggplant	2 tablespoons sugar
½ cup plus 2 tablespoons olive or salad oil	2 tablespoons drained capers
2½ cups sliced onion	½ teaspoon salt
1 cup diced celery	Dash pepper
2 cans (8-oz size) tomato sauce	12 pitted black olives, cut in slivers
¼ cup red-wine vinegar	Toast rounds

1. Wash eggplant; cut into ½-inch cubes.
2. In ½ cup hot oil in large skillet, sauté eggplant until tender and golden-brown. Remove eggplant, and set aside.
3. In 2 tablespoons hot oil in same skillet, sauté onion and celery until tender—about 5 minutes.
4. Return eggplant to skillet. Stir in tomato sauce; bring to boiling. Lower heat, and simmer, covered, 15 minutes.
5. Add vinegar, sugar, capers, salt, pepper, and olives. Simmer, covered, and stirring occasionally, 20 minutes longer.
6. Refrigerate, covered, overnight.
7. To serve: Turn into serving bowl. Surround with toast rounds.

MAKES 8 ANTIPASTO SERVINGS.

Pickled Garden Relish

½ small head cauliflower, cut in flowerets and sliced	1 jar (3 oz) pitted green olives, drained
2 carrots, pared, cut in 2-inch strips	¾ cup wine vinegar
2 stalks celery, cut in 1-inch pieces (1 cup)	½ cup olive or salad oil
1 green pepper, cut in 2-inch strips	2 tablespoons sugar
1 jar (4 oz) pimiento, drained, cut in strips	1 teaspoon salt
	½ teaspoon dried oregano leaves
	¼ teaspoon pepper

1. In large skillet, combine ingredients with ¼ cup water. Bring to boil; stir occasionally. Reduce heat; simmer, covered, 5 minutes.
2. Cool; then refrigerate at least 24 hours.
3. Drain well.

MAKES 8 ANTIPASTO SERVINGS.

Peaches in Marsala

2 cans (1-lb, 14-oz size) peach halves	1 cup cream Marsala
	2 (1-inch) cinnamon sticks

1. Drain the peach halves, reserving 2 tablespoons of the peach syrup.
2. In large bowl, combine peaches, Marsala, cinnamon stick, and reserved syrup.

3. Refrigerate, covered, until the peaches are very well chilled—at least 2 hours.
4. To serve: Turn peaches and liquid into individual dessert dishes.

MAKES 8 SERVINGS.

Pine Nut Cookies

½ cup granulated sugar	1 can (8 oz) almond paste
½ cup confectioners' sugar	2 egg whites, slightly beaten
¼ cup unsifted all-purpose flour	1 jar (3 oz) Italian pignolias
⅛ teaspoon salt	Confectioners' sugar

1. Preheat oven to 300F. Lightly grease 2 large cookie sheets. Sift sugars with flour, salt; set aside.
2. In medium bowl, break up almond paste with wooden spoon. Add egg whites, and beat until well blended and fairly smooth. Stir in flour mixture until well blended.
3. Drop mixture by slightly rounded teaspoonful, 2 inches apart, on prepared cookie sheets. Lightly press into rounds 1½ inches in diameter. Press some pignolias into each.
4. Bake 20 to 25 minutes, or until golden. Remove to wire rack; cool. Sprinkle with confectioners' sugar.

MAKES ABOUT 2½ DOZEN.

OLD-WORLD LASAGNA

Tomato Sauce, right
1 tablespoon salt
1 tablespoon olive
  or salad oil
½ pkg (1-lb size)
  lasagna noodles
1 lb ricotta cheese
1 lb Mozzarella
  cheese, thinly
  sliced
1 jar (3 oz) grated
  Parmesan cheese

1. Make Tomato Sauce as the recipe at right directs.

2. Meanwhile, in large kettle, bring 3 quarts water and the salt to boiling. Add the olive oil.

3. Add lasagna noodles, 2 or 3 pieces at a time, to the boiling water; then return water to boiling.

4. Cook noodles, uncovered, 15 minutes, stirring occasionally.

5. Drain; rinse under hot water.

6. Preheat the oven to 350F. Grease a 13-by-9-by-2-inch baking dish.

7. To assemble lasagna: Spoon a little of tomato sauce evenly into bottom of prepared dish. Over sauce, layer a third each of noodles, ricotta, sauce, Mozzarella, and Parmesan.

8. Repeat layering twice, beginning with noodles and ending with Parmesan.

9. Bake, uncovered, 45 to 50 minutes, or until the cheese is melted and the top is browned.

10. Let lasagna stand 10 to 15 minutes before cutting, to make serving easier. MAKES 8 SERVINGS.

Tomato Sauce

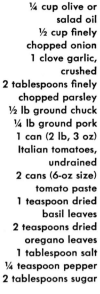

¼ cup olive or
  salad oil
½ cup finely
  chopped onion
1 clove garlic,
  crushed
2 tablespoons finely
  chopped parsley
½ lb ground chuck
¼ lb ground pork
1 can (2 lb, 3 oz)
  Italian tomatoes,
  undrained
2 cans (6-oz size)
  tomato paste
1 teaspoon dried
  basil leaves
2 teaspoons dried
  oregano leaves
1 tablespoon salt
¼ teaspoon pepper
2 tablespoons sugar

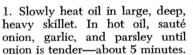

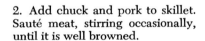

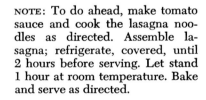

1. Slowly heat oil in large, deep, heavy skillet. In hot oil, sauté onion, garlic, and parsley until onion is tender—about 5 minutes.

2. Add chuck and pork to skillet. Sauté meat, stirring occasionally, until it is well browned.

3. Add rest of sauce ingredients to skillet; stir to mix well. Bring to boiling; reduce heat, and simmer, covered, 3 hours. Stir sauce occasionally during cooking.

NOTE: To do ahead, make tomato sauce and cook the lasagna noodles as directed. Assemble lasagna; refrigerate, covered, until 2 hours before serving. Let stand 1 hour at room temperature. Bake and serve as directed.

Guests for Sunday Supper

This menu makes a light but delicious meal to serve when you are entertaining a small number of close friends on a weekend.

Preparing a soufflé for company has always been a rather hazardous undertaking since a soufflé must come to the table the moment it is ready—it cannot wait for late arrivals. To remove the risk of serving a sunken soufflé, we have developed our own special method of advance preparation.

Make the soufflé as directed through step 10, when the mixture is turned into the prepared soufflé dish. Refrigerate until baking time. The soufflé will hold up to 4 hours. When your last guests have arrived, bake the soufflé as directed. Increase the baking time 12 to 15 minutes since it will be very cold from refrigeration. Naturally, this system works best when you are entertaining a small number of people rather than a very large group.

GUESTS FOR SUNDAY SUPPER
(*Planned for Four*)

*Honeydew Melon Wedges
with Thin Slices of Baked Ham*

*Fabulous Cheese Soufflé
Pan-broiled Tomato Halves*

Miniature Danish Pastries

Hot Rolls   Butter   Preserves

White Wine   Coffee

Honeydew Melon Wedges with Thin Slices of Baked Ham

1 ripe honeydew melon, chilled	4 slices lime
4 slices baked Virginia ham	Mint sprigs

1. Cut honeydew into 4 wedges; remove seeds.
2. Roll ham slices. Place one slice on each melon wedge.
3. Garnish each with a slice of lime and a mint sprig.

MAKES 4 SERVINGS.

Pan-Broiled Tomato Halves

3 large tomatoes (1½ lb)	2 tablespoons packaged dry
1½ teaspoons seasoned salt	bread crumbs
¼ teaspoon pepper	2 tablespoons chopped green
1 tablespoon sugar	onion
¼ cup butter or margarine	

1. Cut out stem end of tomatoes; cut tomatoes in half crosswise.
2. Combine seasoned salt, pepper, and sugar; mix well. Sprinkle evenly over cut sides of tomatoes.
3. In hot butter in large skillet, sauté tomato halves, cut sides down, about 2 minutes, or until soft but not mushy.
4. Turn tomatoes. Baste with pan juices, and sprinkle with bread crumbs. Cook 1 minute longer.
5. With slotted utensil, remove tomatoes to serving platter; sprinkle green onion over top.

MAKES 6 SERVINGS.

Miniature Danish Pastries

1 pkg (14 oz) refrigerator turnover pastries* (cherry, raspberry, blueberry, or apple filling)	1 egg yolk

1. Preheat oven to 400F. Separate half of dough into 4 squares; refrigerate remaining dough.
2. On lightly floured surface, fold each square of dough in half. Roll each into a 5-by-2½-inch rectangle. Cut each rectangle in half to make 2 (2½-inch) squares. Repeat with other 3 squares and with other half of dough, to make 16 squares in all.
3. Shape and fill as directed below. Place on ungreased cookie sheet.
4. Beat egg yolk with 1 teaspoon water; brush over pastries. Bake 10 minutes, or until golden-brown. Serve pastries warm from the oven.

MAKES 16 MINIATURE PASTRIES.

* Or use frozen Danish pastry with various fillings; heat as package label directs.

NOTE: Store frosting from package in refrigerator. Use to frost cookies, if desired.

How to Shape and Fill
Miniature Danish Pastries
Pinwheels

Use a 2½-inch pastry square. Make cuts from tip of each corner to within ½ inch of the center. Squeeze about 1 teaspoon filling in center of each. Bring every other point to the center; moisten slightly, and press together.

Diamonds

Use a 2½-inch pastry square. Squeeze about 1 teaspoon filling in center. Bring two opposite corners to center; moisten slightly, and press edges together.

Tartlets

Use a 2½-inch pastry square. Squeeze about 1 teaspoon filling in center. Bring four corners to center, and press edges together (corners will open slightly during baking).

FABULOUS CHEESE SOUFFLÉ

6 eggs
Butter or margarine
Grated Parmesan
   cheese
6 tablespoons
   unsifted all-purpose
   flour
1½ teaspoons salt
Dash cayenne
1¼ cups milk
½ cup coarsely
   grated natural
   Swiss cheese
¼ teaspoon
   cream of tartar

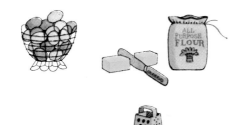

1. Separate eggs, placing whites in large bowl, yolks in another large bowl. Set aside until whites warm to room temperature—about 1 hour.

2. Meanwhile, butter a 1½-quart, straight-side soufflé dish (7½ inches in diameter). Dust lightly with Parmesan—about 1 tablespoon.

3. Tear off a sheet of waxed paper, 26 inches long. Fold lengthwise into thirds. Lightly butter one side.

4. Wrap waxed paper around soufflé dish, with buttered side against dish and a 2-inch rim extending above top edge. Tie with string.

5. Preheat the oven to 350F.

6. Melt 5 tablespoons butter in a medium saucepan; remove from heat. Stir in flour, 1 teaspoon salt, and the cayenne until smooth. Gradually stir in the milk.

7. Bring to boiling, stirring. Reduce heat, and simmer, stirring constantly, until mixture becomes very thick and begins to leave the bottom and side of the pan.

8. With wire whisk or wooden spoon, beat egg yolks. Gradually beat in cooked mixture. Add ½ cup Parmesan cheese and the Swiss cheese; beat until well combined.

9. Add remaining ½ teaspoon salt and the cream of tartar to egg whites. With portable electric mixer at high speed, beat until stiff peaks form when beater is raised.

10. With wire whisk or rubber scraper, fold one third of beaten egg whites into warm cheese mixture until well combined. Carefully fold in remaining egg whites just until combined. Turn into prepared dish.

11. Bake 40 minutes, or until soufflé is puffed and golden-brown. Remove collar. Serve soufflé at once.

MAKES 4 SERVINGS.

A Cocktail Party Buffet

The cocktail party, like other forms of entertaining, has undergone a change. Today, rather than offering an array of small tidbits, the hostess usually provides a more substantial menu, a cocktail buffet which takes the place of a light supper. The reward of serving good food as well as good drinks is a livelier, gayer party; your guests, feeling relaxed and congenial, will stay longer because they are having a good time.

For the menu itself, have three or four of the quiches Lorraine made ahead of time and refrigerated, to be baked as needed. Double the recipe for the rumaki or serve the Swedish meatballs in addition. The rumaki may be prepared in advance, ready for broiling at the last minute; the Swedish meatballs may be completely made ahead and just heated for serving. The rest of the menu, including the ham, is served cold.

As the party comes to an end, serve cups of strong, hot coffee before guests start off on the long trip home.

A COCKTAIL PARTY BUFFET
(Planned for Twenty)

Caviar-Cream-Cheese Ball
Pumpernickel Party Rounds

Rumaki OR *Swedish Meatballs*
Quiche Lorraine

Glazed Baked Ham
Buttered French Bread Slices

Spiced Olives   *Assorted Nuts*

Cocktails   *Coffee*

Caviar-Cream-Cheese Ball

2 pkg (8-oz size) cream cheese	Party pumpernickel slices
1 jar (4 oz) red caviar, slightly drained	

1. Let cream cheese stand at room temperature, to soften—about 1 hour. Then, on serving tray, shape into a mound about 5 inches in diameter; flatten top. Refrigerate, covered.
2. To serve: Spoon caviar over top of cream cheese, letting a little drizzle over side. Surround with pumpernickel.
MAKES 30 SERVINGS.

Rumaki

16 chicken livers	16 slices bacon, halved crosswise
1 cup soy sauce	
½ cup cream sherry	

1. Wash chicken livers; dry well on paper towels.
2. Cut each liver in half, removing any stringy portion. Turn livers into a large bowl.
3. Combine soy sauce and sherry; mix well. Pour over chicken livers; toss lightly to mix well.
4. Wrap each halved chicken liver with half a bacon slice; secure with wooden pick. Arrange on broiler rack in broiler pan. Brush each side with soy mixture.
5. Broil, 3 inches from heat, 2 or 3 minutes on each side, turning once or twice, until bacon is crisp and livers are cooked through.
MAKES 32.

Swedish Meatballs

4 eggs, slightly beaten	Dill weed
2 cups milk	¼ teaspoon allspice
1 cup packaged dry bread crumbs	¼ teaspoon nutmeg
4 tablespoons butter or margarine	¼ teaspoon ground cardamom
1 cup finely chopped onions	⅓ cup flour
2 lb ground chuck	¼ teaspoon pepper
½ lb ground pork	2 cans (10½-oz size) condensed beef broth, undiluted
Salt	1 cup light cream

1. In a large bowl, combine the eggs, milk, and dry bread crumbs.
2. In 2 tablespoons hot butter in large skillet, sauté chopped onion until soft—about 5 minutes. Lift out with slotted spoon. Add to bread-crumb mixture, along with ground meats, 3 teaspoons salt, ½ teaspoon dill weed, the allspice, nutmeg, and cardamom. With a wooden spoon or your hands, mix well to combine.
3. Refrigerate, covered, for 1 hour.
4. Shape meat mixture into 60 meatballs.
5. Preheat the oven to 325F.
6. In remaining hot butter, sauté meatballs, about one-third at a time, until browned all over. Remove as browned to two 2-quart casseroles.
7. Remove the skillet from heat. Pour off all but ¼ cup drippings; stir in flour, ½ teaspoon salt, and the pepper. Gradually stir in beef broth. Bring to boil, stirring constantly. Add cream and 1 teaspoon dill weed. Pour over meatballs in casseroles.
8. Bake, covered, 30 minutes. Garnish top of meatballs with fresh dill sprigs, if desired.
MAKES 20 SERVINGS.

Glazed Baked Ham

¼ cup butter or margarine	2 cups ruby port
2 carrots, sliced	10- to 12-lb fully cooked, bone-in whole ham
2 stalks celery, sliced	
2 medium onions, sliced	½ cup packaged dry bread crumbs
2 parsley sprigs	
3 whole black peppers	¼ cup light-brown sugar, firmly packed
3 whole cloves	

1. Preheat oven to 325F.
2. In hot butter in large, shallow roasting pan, sauté carrot, celery, onion, and parsley until golden—about 5 minutes.
3. Add black peppers, cloves, and port; bring just to boiling, stirring. Remove from heat.
4. Place ham, fat side up, on top of vegetable mixture. Insert meat thermometer in center; do not let it rest on bone. Cover roasting pan tightly with foil.
5. Bake ham, covered, 1½ hours, basting every 20 minutes with wine mixture in pan.
6. Remove foil; continue baking, basting frequently, until thermometer registers 130F—about 1½ hours longer.
7. Remove the ham from the oven. Increase the oven temperature to 400F.
8. Pour off liquid from roasting pan; strain; skim off fat, and reserve liquid.
9. Remove skin and excess fat from ham; score surface in diamond pattern.
10. Combine bread crumbs and sugar. Sprinkle over ham; then press crumb mixture into surface with back of spoon.
11. Bake ham, uncovered, 15 minutes. Spoon reserved liquid over ham; bake 15 minutes longer, or until golden-brown.
12. Remove ham to wire rack. Serve slightly warm or cold. (Rescore ham, to emphasize diamond pattern, if desired.)
MAKES ABOUT 40 SERVINGS.

Spiced Olives

1 jar (9½ oz) unpitted, large green olives	1 clove garlic, minced
½ cup red-wine vinegar	¼ cup finely chopped onion
¼ cup salad oil	1 teaspoon dried oregano leaves
¼ teaspoon crushed red pepper	

1. Turn olives and their liquid into a quart jar with tight-fitting lid.
2. Add vinegar and rest of ingredients; cover tightly; shake well.
3. Refrigerate several days, shaking jar occasionally.
MAKES ABOUT 30.

QUICHE LORRAINE

Pie Shell

½ pkg (9½- to 11-oz size)
  piecrust mix
1 tablespoon soft
  butter

1. Make piecrust mix as the package label directs, sprinkling some of water over all of pastry mixing, tossing it lightly with a fork after each addition, and pushing dampened portion of the mixture to the side.

2. Shape the pastry into a ball. Then wrap it in waxed paper, and refrigerate until you are ready to make pie shell.
3. On lightly floured surface, roll the pastry to an 11-inch circle; roll with light strokes, from the center out to the edge, alternating the directions.

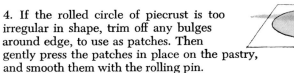

4. If the rolled circle of piecrust is too irregular in shape, trim off any bulges around edge, to use as patches. Then gently press the patches in place on the pastry, and smooth them with the rolling pin.

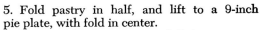

5. Fold pastry in half, and lift to a 9-inch pie plate, with fold in center.
6. Now unfold the pastry, and fit it very carefully into the pie plate.

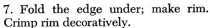

7. Fold the edge under; make rim. Crimp rim decoratively.
8. Spread bottom of the pie shell with butter. Refrigerate until using.

Swiss-Cheese Filling

½ lb sliced bacon
1½ cups grated
  natural Swiss
  cheese (6 oz)
3 eggs
1½ cups light cream
¾ teaspoon salt
Dash nutmeg
Dash cayenne
Dash black pepper

1. Preheat the oven to 375F.

2. Fry bacon until it's crisp; drain on paper towels. Crumble into bits, and sprinkle over bottom of the pie shell.

3. Sprinkle grated cheese over bacon.

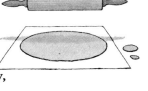

4. In medium bowl, with rotary beater, beat eggs with cream, salt, nutmeg, cayenne, and black pepper until mixture is well combined, but not frothy.
5. Place pie shell on middle shelf in oven. Pour egg mixture into pie shell.

6. Bake 35 to 40 minutes, or until the top is golden and center is firm when it is gently pressed with a fingertip.

7. Let cool on a wire rack for 10 minutes before serving. MAKES 12 HORS D'OEUVRE SERVINGS.

POTS DE CRÈME

Vanilla Crème

3 cups heavy cream
½ cup sugar
1 tablespoon
  vanilla extract
5 egg yolks
Chocolate Curls,
  at right

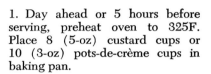

1. Day ahead or 5 hours before serving, preheat oven to 325F. Place 8 (5-oz) custard cups or 10 (3-oz) pots-de-crème cups in baking pan.

2. In medium saucepan, combine cream and sugar; cook over medium heat, stirring occasionally, until sugar is dissolved and mixture is hot. Remove saucepan from heat, and stir in vanilla.

3. In medium bowl, with wire whisk or rotary beater, beat egg yolks until blended but not frothy. Gradually add hot cream mixture, stirring constantly.

4. Strain, using fine strainer, into 4-cup measure. (If desired, first line strainer with cheesecloth.) Pour into cups.

5. Set baking pan on oven rack. Pour hot water to ½-inch level around cups.

6. Bake 25 to 30 minutes, or until mixture just begins to set around edges. (Tilt cup; edge will be firm, center soft.)

7. Immediately remove cups from water, and place on wire rack. Let cool 30 minutes; then refrigerate, each covered with plastic film, foil, or a lid, until well chilled—at least 4 hours.

8. To serve: Top each with sweetened whipped cream, if desired.

Then garnish each serving with a few Chocolate Curls.
MAKES 8 OR 10 SERVINGS.

Chocolate Crème

3 cups heavy cream
½ cup sugar
1½ squares unsweetened
  chocolate,
  broken
1 teaspoon vanilla
  extract
4 egg yolks
Chocolate Curls,
  below

Make and bake as in Vanilla Crème, above, adding chocolate to cream and sugar in step 2. Cook, stirring, until chocolate is melted and mixture is hot.

Coffee Crème

3 cups heavy cream
½ cup sugar
1 tablespoon instant-
  coffee powder
1 teaspoon vanilla
  extract
5 egg yolks
Chocolate Curls,
  below

Make and bake as in Vanilla Crème, above, adding instant coffee to cream and sugar.

Chocolate Curls

Let a 1-oz square semisweet or unsweetened chocolate stand in paper wrapper in warm place about 15 minutes, just to soften slightly. For large curls, unwrap chocolate, and carefully draw vegetable parer across broad, flat surface of square. For smaller curls, draw parer across side of square. Lift curls with a wooden pick, to avoid breaking.

ICE-CREAM BOMBE JUBILEE

Ice-Cream Bombe

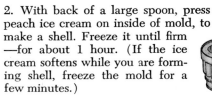

1 qt slightly
soft peach
ice cream
1 qt vanilla
ice cream
1 (7-inch) bakers'
sponge-cake layer
1 cup heavy cream,
whipped

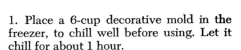

1. Place a 6-cup decorative mold in the freezer, to chill well before using. Let it chill for about 1 hour.

2. With back of a large spoon, press peach ice cream on inside of mold, to make a shell. Freeze it until firm —for about 1 hour. (If the ice cream softens while you are forming shell, freeze the mold for a few minutes.)

3. Fill center of mold with vanilla ice cream, pressing down firmly. Cover with waxed paper. Freeze about 3 hours, or until ice cream is firm.

4. To unmold: Wipe the mold with hot, damp cloth. Invert onto the cake layer on sheet of foil. Then shake out ice cream.

5. Freezer-wrap the bombe; then store it in the freezer until serving time.

6. Just before serving the bombe, make Cherries Jubilee, at the right.

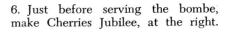
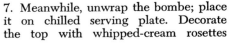

7. Meanwhile, unwrap the bombe; place it on chilled serving plate. Decorate the top with whipped-cream rosettes

Cherries Jubilee

1 can (1 lb, 14 oz)
pitted Bing
cherries
½ cup sugar
1 teaspoon cornstarch
¼ cup brandy

(whipped cream put through pastry bag with a rosette tip). Let bombe stand at room temperature for 5 minutes, to soften slightly.

8. Ignite Cherries Jubilee, and serve them, flaming, over Ice-Cream Bombe. The recipe makes 10 servings.

To make Cherries Jubilee
(see ingredients above):

1. Drain cherries, reserving 1 cup of the syrup.

2. In a small saucepan, combine the sugar and cornstarch; mix well. Then stir in the reserved cherry syrup.

3. Bring the cherry-syrup mixture just to boiling, stirring it constantly. Reduce heat, and simmer for 1 minute longer. (The finished mixture should be slightly thickened, and it should appear translucent.)

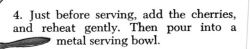

4. Just before serving, add the cherries, and reheat gently. Then pour into a metal serving bowl.

5. Also, heat the brandy, over very low heat, just until vapor rises. Pour brandy over cherries, and ignite.

CHRISTMAS BAKED ALASKA

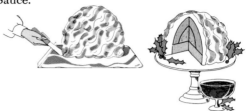

2 pints pistachio ice cream
1½ pints strawberry ice cream

Cardinal Sauce, at right

Meringue:
8 egg whites
½ teaspoon cream
  of tartar
¼ teaspoon salt
1 cup sugar
1 (8-inch) yellow-cake layer

1. Refrigerate a 1½-quart bowl at least ½ hour. Remove pistachio ice cream from freezer, and place on shelf in refrigerator, to soften slightly —about ½ hour if the ice cream is frozen very hard.

2. With large spoon, press pistachio ice cream firmly and evenly around side of chilled bowl. Place in freezer until firm—about ½ hour. Meanwhile, let strawberry ice cream soften in refrigerator.

3. Press strawberry ice cream into center of bowl, smoothing top. Cover with plastic film or foil. Place in freezer, and freeze until firm—several hours or overnight.

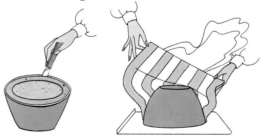

4. To unmold: With a small spatula, loosen ice cream from side of bowl. Invert onto cookie sheet; place a hot, damp dishcloth over bowl; shake gently to release. Immediately return to freezer until firm—at least 2 hours.

5. Meanwhile, make Cardinal Sauce.

6. About 1 hour before serving, let the egg whites warm to room temperature—about 45 minutes.

7. Preheat oven to 425F.

8. Make Meringue: In large bowl, with electric mixer at high speed, beat egg whites with cream of tartar and salt until soft peaks form when beater is slowly raised.

9. Gradually beat in sugar, 2 tablespoons at a time. Continue beating until stiff peaks form when beater is raised.

10. Place sheet of foil on cookie sheet. Arrange the cake layer in center. With broad spatula, place ice cream on cake.

11. With small spatula, spread meringue over ice cream and cake, spreading it down onto foil all around, to seal completely. Make swirls with spatula.

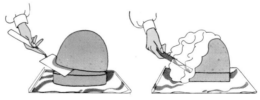

12. Bake, on lowest shelf of oven, 8 to 10 minutes, or until meringue is golden.

13. With small spatula dipped in warm water, carefully loosen meringue from foil; with broad spatula, remove Alaska to serving plate. Decorate with fresh holly, if desired. Serve with Cardinal Sauce.

MAKES 12 SERVINGS.

Cardinal Sauce

1 pkg (10 oz) frozen strawberries, thawed
1 pkg (10 oz) frozen raspberries, thawed
2 teaspoons cornstarch
1 teaspoon lemon juice
½ cup red-currant jelly

1. Turn strawberries and raspberries into a sieve held over a medium saucepan. Let drain. Set berries aside.

2. Combine cornstarch and lemon juice with berry liquid in saucepan.

3. Bring to boiling, stirring; boil gently 1 minute. Add currant jelly; stir until melted.

4. Remove jelly mixture from heat. Stir in berries. Refrigerate, covered, until well chilled—at least 2 hours.

MAKES ABOUT 2¾ CUPS.

OLD-FASHIONED STRAWBERRY SHORTCAKE

Shortcake

2 cups unsifted all-
    purpose flour
¼ cup
    granulated sugar
3 teaspoons baking
    powder
½ teaspoon
    salt
½ cup
    butter or regular margarine
¾ cup milk

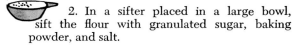

1. Turn oven to 450F. Lightly grease an 8-by-8-by-2-inch square baking pan.

2. In a sifter placed in a large bowl, sift the flour with granulated sugar, baking powder, and salt.

3. Cut butter into chunks; add to flour mixture. With pastry blender, or two knives used scissors fashion, cut in butter until it is in very small particles, all coated with flour mixture. Mixture will resemble coarse cornmeal.

4. Make a well in center of mixture. Pour in milk all at once; mix quickly, with fork, just to moisten flour. Do not overmix; there will be lumps in the dough.

5. Turn into prepared pan, scraping out bowl with rubber scraper. With fingers (dipped in a little flour), lightly press out dough so that it fits corners of the pan and is even in the pan.

6. Bake 15 minutes, or until golden. Cake tester inserted in center comes out clean. Meanwhile, fix berries.

7. Loosen edges with a sharp knife; then turn out on a wire rack.

Strawberry Topping

3 pint boxes fresh
    strawberries
¾ cup granulated
    sugar
1 cup heavy
    cream
2 tablespoons
    confectioners'
    sugar

1. Wash strawberries in cold water; drain. Choose several of the nicest berries for garnish, and set them aside.

2. Then remove hulls from rest of berries; slice berries into a bowl. Add granulated sugar; mix well. Set berries aside until shortcake is ready.

3. To serve: Beat cream, with a rotary beater, just until it is stiff. Gently stir in confectioners' sugar.

4. Using serrated-edge knife, carefully cut cake in half crosswise. Put bottom, cut side up, on serving plate. Spoon over half of sliced berries.

5. Set top of cake in place, cut side down. Spoon rest of sliced berries over top of cake. Mound whipped cream lightly in center. Garnish with whole strawberries. Serve at once. MAKES 8 SERVINGS.

PINEAPPLE UPSIDE-DOWN CAKE

2 cans (8¼-oz size) sliced pineapple
(8 slices)
¼ cup butter or margarine
⅔ cup light-brown sugar,
firmly packed
8 maraschino cherries, drained
¼ cup pecan halves
or broken walnuts
1 cup sifted all-purpose flour
¾ cup granulated sugar
1½ teaspoons baking powder
½ teaspoon salt
¼ cup shortening
½ cup milk
1 egg
Whipped cream

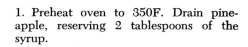

1. Preheat oven to 350F. Drain pineapple, reserving 2 tablespoons of the syrup.

2. Melt butter in a 10-inch heavy skillet, over low heat. Add brown sugar, stirring until sugar is melted. Remove from heat.

3. Arrange drained pineapple on sugar mixture in skillet. Fill centers of pineapple slices with cherries and spaces between slices with pecans. Set skillet aside.

4. Into medium bowl, sift flour with granulated sugar, baking powder, and salt. Add shortening and milk. With electric mixer at medium speed, beat 2 minutes.

5. Add egg and reserved pineapple syrup; beat 2 minutes longer. Pour cake batter over pineapple in skillet, spreading evenly.

6. Bake 40 to 45 minutes, or until cake springs back when gently pressed with fingertip.

7. Let stand on wire rack just 5 minutes. With small spatula, loosen cake from edge of skillet. Cover with serving plate; invert; shake gently; then lift off pan.

8. Serve the cake warm. Top individual servings with whipped cream. Or top with small spoonful of vanilla ice cream, if desired.

MAKES 8 SERVINGS.

APRICOT UPSIDE-DOWN CAKE

Make and bake as above, substituting 1 can (1 lb, 1 oz) unpeeled apricot halves, drained well on paper towels, for sliced pineapple and syrup from apricots for pineapple syrup. Arrange apricots, cut side up, on brown-sugar mixture, and surround with cherries and nuts.

PEACH UPSIDE-DOWN CAKE

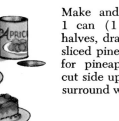

Make and bake as above, substituting 1 can (1 lb, 1 oz) cling-peach slices, well drained, for sliced pineapple and syrup from peaches for pineapple syrup. Arrange peach slices, cherries, and nuts decoratively on the brown-sugar mixture.

UPSIDE-DOWN CAKE WITH CAKE MIX

Make any of fruit toppings in skillet, as directed above. Then prepare a package of 2-layer yellow-cake mix as label directs. Measure 2½ cups batter, and pour over fruit. Turn remaining batter into greased and floured 8-inch layer-cake pan, and bake along with upside-down cake. If desired, freeze plain layer for dessert another day.

HOLIDAY WHITE FRUITCAKE

Fruit Mixture

1 lb blanched whole
   almonds
2 jars (3½-oz size)
   candied red cherries
1 jar (3½-oz)
   candied green cherries
2 jars (4-oz size)
   diced candied citron
2 jars (4-oz size)
   diced candied
   pineapple
1 jar (4 oz) diced
   candied orange peel
½ lb golden raisins
½ cup unsifted all-
   purpose flour

White Batter

1¼ cups butter
   or margarine, softened
1½ cups sugar
¼ teaspoon salt
 4 eggs
½ cup milk
¼ cup sherry
¾ teaspoon almond
   extract
2½ cups sifted all-
   purpose flour

Sherry or brandy

1. Line a 10-inch tube pan: On a piece of brown paper, draw an 18-inch circle, and cut out. Set pan in center of circle; draw around base of pan and tube. With pencil lines outside, fold paper circle into eighths. Snip off tip. Unfold circle; cut along folds just to second circle. Grease both the pan and paper well; fit the paper, greased side up, into tube pan.

2. Prepare Fruit Mixture: With a very sharp knife, coarsely cut up almonds. Cut cherries in half.

3. In very large bowl, combine nuts, fruits, and ½ cup unsifted flour; mix well. Preheat oven to 275F.

4. Make White Batter: In large bowl of electric mixer, at medium speed, beat butter until creamy. Gradually add sugar, beating until light—about 5 minutes.

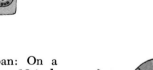
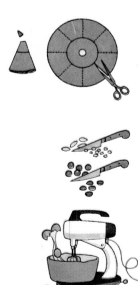

5. Add salt. Then add eggs, one at a time, beating after each addition; beat until light and fluffy.

6. Mix the milk, ¼ cup sherry, and the almond extract.

7. At low speed, alternately blend into sugar-egg mixture the sifted flour (in fourths) and the milk-and-sherry mixture (in thirds), beginning and ending with flour. Beat only until blended.

8. Pour batter over fruit mixture. With hands or wooden spoon, mix until well combined.

9. Turn into prepared tube pan, packing firmly. Bake cake 3 hours, or until a cake tester inserted in the center comes out clean.

10. Cool cake in pan 1 hour. Remove from pan; invert on rack, and peel off paper. Cool completely.

11. Soak large piece of cheesecloth in ⅓ cup sherry or brandy. Use to wrap fruitcake. Overwrap in plastic film or foil. Store in refrigerator.

12. Store the fruitcake at least 4 weeks, to develop flavor. Resoak cheesecloth in sherry as needed.

13. Before serving, decorate, if desired, as below. Slice into thin pieces.

Decoration

1. Between two sheets of waxed paper, roll 1 can (8 oz) almond paste into an 8-inch circle; remove top sheet of paper. Invert almond paste onto top of cake; remove paper. With sharp knife, trim edge. Press paste to cake.

2. Combine 1⅓ cups sifted confectioners' sugar, 2 tablespoons melted butter or margarine, 1½ tablespoons milk, and ¼ teaspoon almond extract; mix until smooth.

3. Spoon over almond paste. With small spatula, smooth frosting, letting it drip down side of cake.

4. Garnish the cake with candied cherries and angelica.

GLAZED LEMON-CREAM-CHEESE CAKE

Crust

2½ cups packaged
   graham-cracker crumbs
¼ cup sugar
½ cup butter
   or regular margarine,
   softened

Filling

3 pkg (8-oz size)
   soft cream cheese
3 tablespoons
   grated lemon peel
1½ cups sugar
3 tablespoons flour
4 eggs
½ cup lemon juice

Dairy sour cream

1. Make Crust: In medium bowl, with hands or back of metal spoon, mix graham-cracker crumbs with sugar and butter until well combined.

2. With back of spoon, press crumb mixture to the bottom and sides of a greased 12-by-8-by-2-inch baking dish.

3. Preheat the oven to 350F.

4. Make Filling: In large bowl of electric mixer, at medium speed, beat cream cheese, grated lemon peel, sugar, and flour until they are smooth and well combined.

5. Beat in eggs, one at a time. Then beat in the lemon juice.

6. Pour filling into crust-lined dish. Bake 35 to 40 minutes, or until center of filling seems firm when dish is shaken.

7. Cool completely on wire rack. Refrigerate 4 hours, or overnight—until it is very well chilled.

8. Meanwhile, make Glazes, at right.

9. Lightly mark filling in half crosswise. Then mark each half diagonally, forming 8 sections in all. Spoon glaze evenly over each section, as shown. Refrigerate 1 hour before cutting into squares to serve. Pass the sour cream. Wonderful for a large buffet or dessert party. Makes 12 to 16 servings.

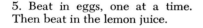

Blueberry Glaze

1 pkg (10 oz) frozen
   blueberries, thawed
1 tablespoon sugar
2 teaspoons cornstarch

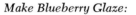

Pineapple Glaze

1 tablespoon sugar
2 teaspoons cornstarch
1 can (8½ oz) crushed
   pineapple, undrained

Strawberry Glaze

1 pkg (10 oz) frozen
   strawberry halves, thawed
1 tablespoon sugar
2 teaspoons cornstarch

Make Blueberry Glaze:

1. Drain blueberries, reserving liquid. Measure liquid; add water, if necessary, to make ½ cup.

2. In small saucepan, combine sugar and cornstarch. Stir in reserved liquid.

3. Over medium heat, bring to boiling, stirring; boil 1 minute.

4. Remove from heat; cool slightly. Stir in the blueberries. Cool completely.

Make Pineapple Glaze:

1. In small saucepan, combine sugar and cornstarch. Stir in pineapple.

2. Over medium heat, bring to boiling, stirring; boil 1 minute. Cool completely.

Make Strawberry Glaze:

1. Drain the strawberries, reserving ½ cup of the liquid.

2. In a small saucepan, combine sugar and cornstarch. Stir in reserved liquid.

3. Over medium heat, bring to boiling, stirring; boil 1 minute.

4. Remove from heat; cool slightly. Stir in strawberries; cool completely.

WALNUT-RAISIN CAKE

1 cup seedless raisins
1 cup walnuts
1 teaspoon baking soda
1 cup boiling water
All-purpose flour
1 teaspoon cinnamon
¼ teaspoon salt
½ cup butter or regular
   margarine
1 cup sugar

1 egg
2 egg yolks
1 teaspoon lemon
   juice
1 teaspoon vanilla
   extract

Butterscotch
   Frosting, below
Walnut halves

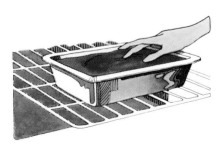

1. Preheat oven to 325F. Grease lightly, with butter, a 9-by-5-by-3-inch loaf pan.

2. Coarsely chop raisins and 1 cup walnuts; place in medium bowl. Add baking soda; then stir in boiling water. Set aside.

3. Sift flour onto sheet of waxed paper. Measure 1½ cups. Sift measured flour with cinnamon and salt. Set aside.

4. In large bowl, with electric mixer at medium speed, beat ½ cup butter till creamy. Add sugar, a little at a time, beating till light and fluffy. Stop beater once or twice; scrape down side of bowl with rubber spatula.

5. Add egg and egg yolks, one at a time, beating after each addition and scraping down side of bowl with rubber spatula. Beat until light and fluffy. Add lemon juice, vanilla.

6. With wooden spoon, beat in flour mixture in fourths, alternately with raisin mixture in thirds, beginning and ending with flour mixture. Pour batter into prepared pan.

7. Bake 1 hour and 15 minutes, or until top springs back when lightly pressed with fingertip and cake has pulled away from pan at edge.

8. Cool in pan on wire rack 5 minutes. With small spatula, loosen around edge. Turn out on wire rack; turn top up; let cool completely.

9. Frost top with Butterscotch Frosting, letting some run down side. Decorate with walnut halves. Or sprinkle cake with confectioners' sugar, if you prefer. To serve, slice in ½-inch-thick slices.

MAKES 14 OR 15 SERVINGS.

Butterscotch Frosting

¼ cup butter or regular margarine
½ cup light-brown sugar, firmly packed
2 tablespoons milk
Dash Salt
¼ teaspoon vanilla extract
¾ cup sifted confectioners' sugar

1. Melt butter in small saucepan. Stir in brown sugar; cook over low heat, stirring, 3 minutes.

2. Slowly stir in milk and salt; bring mixture to boiling, stirring constantly.

3. Remove from heat. Let cool to lukewarm—this will take about 30 minutes.

4. Stir in vanilla. Beat in confectioners' sugar, a small amount at a time, and continue beating until frosting is thick enough to spread.

DEEP-DISH FRUIT PIE

Deep-dish Peach Pie

½ pkg (9½- to 11-oz size)
   piecrust mix
2½ to 3 lb fresh peaches
¾ cup light-brown sugar,
   firmly packed
3 tablespoons flour
⅛ teaspoon salt
Dash ground cloves
Dash nutmeg
⅓ cup heavy cream
2 tablespoons lemon juice
2 tablespoons butter or
   margarine
1 egg yolk
Heavy cream or
   vanilla ice cream

1. Prepare piecrust mix, as package label directs, for one-crust pie. Shape dough into ball; flatten; wrap or place in small plastic bag, and refrigerate until ready to use.

2. Peel peaches, using a vegetable parer. Halve each. Remove pits, and slice peaches to make 6 cups.

3. In small bowl, combine brown sugar, flour, salt, cloves, and nutmeg. Stir in ⅓ cup cream.

4. Place sliced peaches in an 8¼-inch round, shallow baking dish or 9-inch deep-dish-pie plate (about 1¾ inches deep). Sprinkle with lemon juice; add cream mixture. With wooden spoon, stir gently until well mixed. Dot with butter.

5. Preheat oven to 400F.

6. On lightly floured surface, roll out pastry to an 11-inch circle. Fold in half; make slits for steam vents.

7. Place over fruit in baking dish, and unfold. Press pastry to edge of dish. For decorative edge, press firmly all around with thumb.

8. Lightly beat egg yolk with 1 tablespoon water. Brush over pastry.

9. Place a piece of foil, a little larger than baking dish, on oven rack below the one on which pie bakes, to catch

any juices that may bubble over edge of dish. Bake pie 35 to 40 minutes, or until crust is golden and juice bubbles through steam vents.

10. Let pie cool on wire rack about 30 minutes. Serve warm, with heavy cream or ice cream.

MAKES 6 TO 8 SERVINGS.

Deep-dish Pear Pie

Make as above, substituting about 2¼ pounds fresh pears for peaches. Halve pears lengthwise. Scoop out core; then cut a V shape, to remove stem. Pare; slice to make 6 cups.

Deep-dish Pie with Canned Fruit

Use 2 cans (1-lb, 13-oz size) sliced cling peaches or 2 cans (1-lb, 13-oz size) sliced pears. Drain, reserving 2 tablespoons syrup. Make as above, reducing sugar to ½ cup and decreasing flour to 2 tablespoons. Add reserved syrup with the cream.

Deep-dish Apple-Cider Pie

1. Make filling: Combine 1½ cups apple cider or juice and 1 to 1¼ cups sugar in large saucepan; bring to boiling; stir until sugar is dissolved. Boil, uncovered, 10 minutes.

2. Pare, quarter, core 3 pounds tart cooking apples. Slice thinly. Sprinkle with 2 tablespoons lemon juice. Add to cider mixture; return to boiling; stir often. Reduce heat; simmer, uncovered, 5 minutes.

3. With slotted spoon, remove apples to 8¼-inch round, shallow baking dish, mounding in center. Return syrup to boiling; boil, uncovered, 5 minutes. Pour over apples. Dot with 2 tablespoons butter.

4. Preheat oven to 400F. Prepare ½ package piecrust mix, as package label directs. Complete as directed in steps 6 to 10 above.

OLD-FASHIONED APPLE PIE

Flaky Pastry

2 cups sifted all-
    purpose flour
1 teaspoon salt
¾ cup shortening
4 to 5 tablespoons
    ice water

Apple Filling

1 cup granulated
    sugar
1 teaspoon cinnamon
¼ cup unsifted all-
    purpose flour
Dash salt
About 2½ lb
    tart cooking apples
2 tablespoons
    butter or margarine

1 egg yolk

1. Make Flaky Pastry: Sift the flour with salt into a medium bowl. With a pastry blender or 2 knives, cut in shortening until mixture resembles coarse cornmeal.

2. Quickly sprinkle ice water, 1 tablespoon at a time, over flour mixture, tossing it lightly with a fork after each addition and pushing dampened portion of the mixture to side of bowl. (Pastry should be just moist enough to hold together, not sticky.) Shape into a ball; halve; flatten each half.

3. Place one half of pastry between two sheets of waxed paper. On dampened counter top (this prevents paper from slipping), roll out pastry to an 11-inch circle, rolling from center out to the edge and alternating direction with each stroke. Repeat with other half.

4. Refrigerate pastry circles, still between paper, for 30 minutes.

5. Preheat the oven to 425F.

6. Make Apple Filling: In a large bowl, combine the sugar, cinnamon, flour, and salt; mix well.

7. Pare, quarter, core, and slice apples. (Apple slices should measure 7 cups.) Add apple to the sugar mixture, and toss lightly.

8. For bottom crust of pie: Peel off top waxed paper from one pastry circle. Invert pastry into a 9-inch pie plate. Peel off other paper. Carefully fit pastry into pie plate, pressing toward center.

9. Turn the apple mixture into pie plate, mounding it in center. Dot the filling with butter. Trim edge even with pie plate, if necessary.

10. Peel off top sheet of waxed paper from remaining pastry circle. Make several slits for steam vents.

11. Invert pastry over filling; peel off paper. Fold top crust under bottom crust; press together, to seal. Crimp edge decoratively.

12. To glaze crust, beat the egg yolk with 1 tablespoon water. Brush mixture over top crust.

13. Bake pie 45 to 50 minutes, or until the apple is tender and the crust is golden-brown.

14. Cool the pie partially on wire rack. Serve warm, with slices of Cheddar cheese if desired.

MAKES 6 TO 8 SERVINGS.

HOT MINCE PIE WITH RUM SAUCE

Rich Pastry

1 pkg (9½ to 11 oz) piecrust mix
1 tablespoon sugar
Ice water
2 tablespoons firm butter

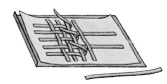

Filling

1 jar (1 lb, 12 oz) prepared mincemeat,
   with brandy and rum
1 cup applesauce
1 cup coarsely chopped walnuts

1 egg yolk

Rum Sauce, at right

1. Make Rich Pastry: In medium bowl, combine piecrust mix and sugar. Blend in water as package label directs. Shape pastry into a ball.

2. On lightly floured surface, roll out pastry to a 15-inch circle. Cut butter into small pieces; dot over pastry.

3. Fold pastry in thirds, one side overlapping the other. Press edges together to seal.

4. Fold again into thirds, from each end; seal (you will have a rectangle about 5 by 4½ inches). Wrap in waxed paper. Refrigerate 30 minutes.

5. Make Filling: In medium bowl, combine mincemeat, applesauce, and walnuts; mix well.

6. Divide chilled pastry in half. Place each half between two sheets of waxed paper. On wet counter top (so paper won't slip), roll out one half of pastry to an 11-inch circle; then roll out other half to a 12-by-6-inch rectangle. Refrigerate 10 minutes, or until pastry is firm enough to handle easily.

7. For bottom crust of pie: Peel top paper from pastry circle. Invert pastry into a 9-inch pie plate; peel off other sheet of paper. Carefully fit pastry into pie plate, pressing gently toward the center of the plate. Refrigerate.

8. Preheat oven to 425F.

9. For the lattice top, peel top paper from

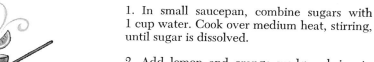

the pastry rectangle. With pastry wheel or sharp knife, trim edges; cut, lengthwise, into 10 strips, ½ inch wide.

10. Place sheet of waxed paper on cookie sheet. Arrange 5 pastry strips, side by side and 1 inch apart, on waxed paper. Weave remaining strips, one at a time and 1 inch apart, over and under first strips. Refrigerate 15 minutes.

11. Turn filling into pastry-lined pie plate. Carefully invert lattice top over filling; peel off paper. Trim ends of strips. Fold edge of lower crust over ends of strips; pinch together. Then press edge of pastry all around with floured tines of fork.

12. Beat egg yolk with 1 tablespoon water. Brush over lattice top but not on edge of pastry.

13. Place double thickness of brown paper (12-inch square) under pie plate. Bake 30 to 35 minutes, or until crust is nicely browned.

14. Meanwhile, make Rum Sauce.

15. Let pie cool slightly on a wire rack. Then cut into wedges, and top with flaming sauce. (Or omit sauce, and serve pie with vanilla ice cream.)

MAKES 8 SERVINGS.

Rum Sauce

⅓ cup granulated sugar
⅓ cup light-brown sugar,
   firmly packed
1 lemon wedge
1 orange wedge
¼ cup dark rum

1. In small saucepan, combine sugars with 1 cup water. Cook over medium heat, stirring, until sugar is dissolved.

2. Add lemon and orange wedges; bring to boiling. Boil, uncovered, 20 minutes. Discard fruit.

3. Just before serving, add rum; heat, over very low heat, just until vapor rises. Remove from heat. Ignite with match; serve over pieces of pie.

NOTE: If you wish, bake pie a day ahead of serving. Let cool; then refrigerate. To serve, place in 325F oven 30 minutes, or just until heated through.

LEMON MERINGUE PIE

Pie Shell:

1½ sticks piecrust mix

Lemon Filling:

1¾ cups sugar
¼ cup cornstarch
3 tablespoons flour
¼ teaspoon salt
4 egg yolks
½ cup lemon juice
1 tablespoon
  grated lemon peel
1 tablespoon
  butter or
  margarine

Meringue:

4 egg whites, at room
  temperature
¼ teaspoon cream of tartar
½ cup sugar

1. Make piecrust mix as the package label directs, using 3 tablespoons liquid called for. Sprinkle liquid, a little at a time, over pastry mixture; toss lightly with a fork after each addition, and push the dampened portion of pastry mixture to side of bowl.

2. Shape the pastry into a ball. Then wrap it in waxed paper, and refrigerate it for 30 minutes, or until you are ready to make pie shell.

3. Between two sheets of waxed paper or on a lightly floured pastry cloth, roll the pastry to a 12-inch circle; roll with light strokes, from the center out to the edge, alternating the directions. (Place waxed paper on a slightly dampened dishcloth, to prevent slipping.)

4. Peel top sheet of waxed paper from pastry circle. Invert pastry into a 9-inch pie plate. Fit it very carefully into the pie plate.

5. Fold the edge under; make rim. Crimp rim decoratively. Prick entire surface well with a fork. Refrigerate the shell 30 minutes.

6. Meanwhile, preheat oven to 450F. Bake shell 8 to 10 minutes, or until golden-brown.

7. Cool pie shell completely on wire rack.

8. Make Lemon Filling: In medium-size, heavy saucepan, combine 1¾ cups sugar with the cornstarch, flour, and salt; mix well. Gradually add 2 cups water, stirring until smooth.

9. Over medium heat, bring mixture to boiling, stirring occasionally, not constantly. Boil 1 minute. Remove from heat. (Constant stirring might break down mixture and make it thin.)

10. In a small bowl, beat egg yolks slightly. Quickly stir in some of hot mixture.

Return to remaining mixture in pan, stirring until blended. Cook over low heat 5 minutes, stirring gently. Remove from heat.

11. Gently mix in lemon juice, lemon peel, and butter. Pour warm mixture into pie shell.

12. Preheat oven to 400F.

13. Make Meringue: In a medium bowl, with electric mixer at medium speed, beat the egg whites with the cream of tartar till frothy.

14. Gradually beat in sugar, 2 tablespoons at a time, beating well after each addition. Beat at high speed till stiff, glossy peaks form when beater is slowly raised.

15. Spread meringue over lemon filling, carefully sealing to edge of the crust. Swirl top decoratively.

16. Bake 7 to 9 minutes, or until meringue is golden-brown. Let pie cool completely on wire rack—3 hours. Refrigerate at least 1 hour.

MAKES 8 SERVINGS.

63

LEMON CHIFFON PIE

1 env unflavored gelatine
4 eggs
½ cup lemon juice
1 cup sugar
¼ teaspoon salt
1 tablespoon grated
   lemon peel
Yellow food color
Graham-Cracker Pie
   Shell, at right
1 cup heavy
   cream

1. Sprinkle gelatine over ¼ cup cold water in measuring cup; set aside to soften.

2. Separate eggs, placing whites in large bowl of electric mixer, yolks in double-boiler top. Set whites aside to warm to room temperature.

3. Beat yolks slightly with wooden spoon. Stir in lemon juice, ½ cup sugar, and salt.

4. Cook over hot, not boiling, water (water shouldn't touch bottom of double-boiler top), stirring constantly, until mixture thickens and coats metal spoon —about 12 minutes.

5. Add gelatine mixture and lemon peel, stirring until gelatine is dissolved. Add 2 drops food color; mix well. Remove pan from hot water. Refrigerate, stirring occasionally, until cool and the consistency of unbeaten egg white—about 35 minutes.

6. Meanwhile, make Graham-Cracker Pie Shell.

7. At high speed, beat egg whites just until soft peaks form when the beater is slowly raised —peaks bend slightly.

8. Gradually beat in remaining ½ cup sugar, 2 tablespoons at a time, beating well after each addition. Continue beating until stiff peaks form when beater is raised.

9. With rubber scraper or wire whisk, gently fold gelatine mixture into egg-white mixture just until combined.

10. Gently turn into the pie shell, mounding high. Refrigerate until firm—3 to 6 hours.

11. To serve: Whip cream until stiff. Spread about half of it over pie. Put remaining cream in pastry bag with number-30 decorating tip, and pipe rosettes around pie edge.

MAKES 6 TO 8 SERVINGS.

Graham-Cracker Pie Shell

1¼ cups packaged
   graham-cracker crumbs
¼ cup sugar
¼ teaspoon
   cinnamon
⅓ cup butter
or regular margarine, softened

1. In medium bowl, combine all ingredients; blend with fork or pastry blender.

2. With back of spoon, press evenly on bottom and side, not rim, of 9-inch pie plate.

3. Refrigerate until using.

CREAM PUFFS

½ cup water
¼ cup butter or regular margarine
⅛ teaspoon salt
½ cup unsifted all-purpose flour
2 large eggs
Custard Filling, at right
Chocolate Glaze, at right
Confectioners' sugar

1. Preheat oven to 400F.

2. In small saucepan, combine water, butter, and salt. Over medium heat, bring to boiling. Remove from heat.

3. Immediately, with wooden spoon, beat in all the flour.

4. Over low heat, beat until mixture leaves side of pan and forms a ball—1 to 2 minutes. Remove from heat.

5. Add 1 egg; with portable electric mixer or wooden spoon, beat until well blended. Then add other egg, and beat until the dough is shiny and satiny—about 1 minute.

6. Drop the dough by rounded table-spoonful, 2 inches apart, onto an ungreased cookie sheet.

7. Bake 35 to 40 minutes, or until puffed and golden-brown. Puffs should sound hollow when lightly tapped with fingertip.

8. Meanwhile, make Custard Filling.

9. Carefully remove puffs to wire rack. Let cool completely, away from drafts.

10. Shortly before serving: Cut off tops of cream puffs with sharp knife. With fork, gently remove any soft dough from the inside.

11. Fill puffs with custard; replace tops. Frost tops with Chocolate Glaze, or sprinkle with confectioners' sugar. Serve soon after filling. (Filled puffs become soggy on standing.)

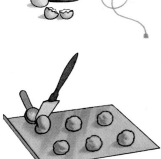

MAKES 6 LARGE PUFFS.

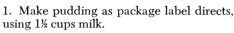

Miniature Cream Puffs: Drop batter by level teaspoonful, 2 inches apart, on ungreased cookie sheet. Bake 20 to 25 minutes at 400F. Proceed as directed at left. Fill and frost for dessert, or fill with savory filling for hors d'oeuvre.

MAKES 36 MINIATURE PUFFS.

Custard Filling

1 pkg (3¼ oz) vanilla-pudding-
and-pie-filling mix
1½ cups milk
½ cup heavy cream
2 tablespoons confectioners' sugar
½ teaspoon vanilla extract

1. Make pudding as package label directs, using 1½ cups milk.

2. Pour into medium bowl; place waxed paper directly on surface. Refrigerate until chilled—at least 1 hour.

3. In small bowl, combine heavy cream, sugar, and vanilla; with rotary beater, beat just until stiff. Then fold whipped-cream mixture into pudding until combined.

4. Refrigerate several hours, to chill well before using.

MAKES 2 CUPS; enough filling for 6 large puffs or 36 miniature puffs.

Chocolate Glaze

½ cup semisweet-chocolate pieces
1 tablespoon shortening
1 tablespoon light
corn syrup
1½ tablespoons milk

1. In top of double boiler, combine the chocolate pieces, shortening, corn syrup, and milk.

2. Place over hot, not boiling, water, stirring occasionally, until mixture is smooth and well blended. Let cool slightly before using to frost puffs.

MAKES ½ CUP.

APPLE DUMPLINGS

- 1 pkg (9½ to 11 oz) piecrust mix
- ¼ teaspoon nutmeg
- 3 tablespoons butter or regular margarine, softened
- 3 tablespoons sugar
- 1 tablespoon dark raisins
- 2 tablespoons chopped walnuts
- ¾ teaspoon cinnamon
- 4 medium baking apples or pears (about 2 lb)
- ½ cup maple-blended syrup

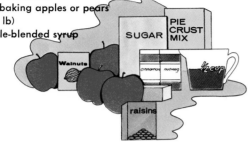

1. Prepare piecrust mix as package label directs. First, stir nutmeg into mix, with a fork. Then, a little at a time, sprinkle over piecrust mix the cold water called for on the package label. Form pastry into a ball; wrap in waxed paper. Place in refrigerator.

2. In small bowl, combine butter, sugar, raisins, chopped walnuts, and cinnamon; mix until they are well blended.

3. Pare and core apples (or pears). Fill each with raisin-walnut mixture.

4. Preheat oven to 375F. Generously grease a 13-by-9-by-2-inch baking dish.

5. Divide pastry into fourths. On lightly floured surface, roll out each part, from center to edge, to make a 7-inch square. Trim edges, using pastry wheel for decorative edge, if desired. Reserve trimmings.

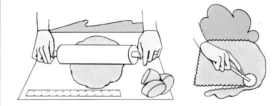

6. Place an apple (or pear) in center of each square. Bring each corner of square to top of apple, and pinch edges of pastry together firmly, to cover apple completely.

7. Reroll trimmings. With leaf-shape cookie cutter, cut out as many leaves as possible. Brush leaves with cold water, and press on top of the dumplings.

8. Arrange dumplings in prepared baking dish. Brush the top and side of each with some of the maple-blended syrup.

9. Bake, brushing occasionally with syrup, 40 minutes, or until pastry is a rich golden-brown and apples seem tender when tested with wooden pick. With broad spatula, immediately remove dumplings to serving dish. They are nice with light cream, soft vanilla ice cream, or hard sauce.

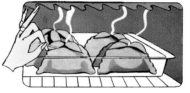

MAKES 4 SERVINGS.

LEMON TARTS

Filling

3 eggs
2 tablespoons grated
   lemon peel
½ cup lemon juice
¾ cup soft butter
1 cup plus 2 tablespoons
   sugar

1 pkg (9½ to 11 oz) piecrust mix
½ cup heavy cream

1. Make Filling: In top of double boiler, beat eggs well with a fork. Add lemon peel and juice, butter, and 1 cup sugar; mix till combined.

2. Place over simmering water (water should not touch bottom of double-boiler top); cook egg-lemon mixture, stirring constantly, about 15 to 20 minutes, or until mixture forms a thick coating on a metal spoon and mounds slightly.

3. Remove mixture from heat, and turn it into a bowl. Refrigerate the filling, covered, several hours, or until it is well chilled.

4. Prepare piecrust mix as package label directs. Form into a ball.

5. Divide pastry ball in half; divide each half into 4 parts.

6. Roll each part, between two sheets of waxed paper, into a 6-inch circle. (Place waxed paper on slightly dampened surface, to prevent slipping.) Use each circle to line a 4-inch fluted tart pan, pressing pastry evenly to bottom and side of each pan. Trim evenly with top of pan. *Or:* If you don't have tart pans, divide pastry into 10 parts. Roll each into a 6-inch circle. Invert a bowl, 5 inches in diameter, over each circle. With knife, cut out 5-inch circles. Fit the circles over outside of 10 inverted 5-ounce custard cups; pinch into pleats, to fit snugly. (Use extra tart shells another time.)

7. Refrigerate the tart shells for 30 minutes. Prick the shells well with a fork before baking.

8. Meanwhile, preheat oven to 450F.

9. Bake tart shells, on large cookie sheet, 10 to 12 minutes, or until they are golden-brown. During baking, prick shells again if pastry buckles from pans.

10. Cool tart shells completely on a wire rack. Then carefully remove them from pans.

11. In a small bowl, using a rotary beater, beat heavy cream with 2 tablespoons sugar until stiff.

12. Divide the lemon filling into 8 tart shells. Decorate the tops with whipped cream, using a spoon or a pastry bag with decorating tip. Sprinkle whipped cream with grated lemon peel, if desired.

MAKES 8 TARTS.

ORANGE TARTS

Substitute 2 tablespoons grated orange peel for lemon peel, ½ cup fresh orange juice for the ½ cup lemon juice. Add 1 tablespoon lemon juice.

LIME TARTS

Substitute 1 tablespoon grated lime peel for the grated lemon peel, and ½ cup lime juice for the lemon juice. Tint a pale green by adding 2 drops green food color.

PINEAPPLE TARTS

Omit the lemon peel, and substitute ½ cup pineapple juice for lemon juice. Add 1 tablespoon lemon juice. When the filling mixture is chilled, gently fold in ¼ cup of drained crushed pineapple.

PETIT-FOUR COOKIES

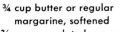

¾ cup butter or regular
  margarine, softened
⅔ cup granulated sugar
¼ teaspoon salt
2 egg yolks
1 tablespoon light cream
1 teaspoon vanilla
  extract
2 cups unsifted all-
  purpose flour

Confectioners' sugar
Raspberry or apricot jam
Chopped walnuts, pistachios,
  or pecans
Sliced blanched almonds
Chocolate shot
Candied cherries
Chocolate Glaze, at right

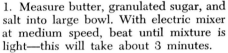

1. Measure butter, granulated sugar, and salt into large bowl. With electric mixer at medium speed, beat until mixture is light—this will take about 3 minutes.

2. Add egg yolks, cream, and vanilla. Beat until the mixture is fluffy—2 minutes.

3. Gradually add flour, stirring with wooden spoon until well combined and dough is smooth.

4. With hands or spoon, shape dough into a ball. Place on waxed paper, plastic film, or foil. Flatten; cut in quarters; wrap each quarter.

5. Refrigerate 2 hours. The dough will be firm.

6. Preheat oven to 325F.

7. On lightly floured pastry cloth, with floured rolling pin, roll out one fourth of dough at a time to about ¼-inch thickness. Gently press together any cracks at edge.

8. Choose shapes, above right, and cut as directed. Place cut cookies, 1 inch apart, on ungreased cookie sheets. (If desired, decorate some of the cookies before baking, as directed at right.)

9. Bake 12 to 15 minutes, or just until edges of cookies are golden.

10. Remove to wire rack; let cool completely. Decorate.

MAKES ABOUT 6½ DOZEN ASSORTED TEA COOKIES.

To Cut Shapes

Rounds, Half-Moons, Crescents, Diamonds: Cut dough with a 1½- or 2-inch plain or scalloped round cookie cutter, for round cookies. Cut rounds in half, for half-moons. Cut dough with a 2-inch crescent-shape cutter and with a 2-inch diamond-shape cutter, for crescents and diamonds.

Ribbons: Roll out dough into a long strip 2½ inches wide and ¼ inch thick. Trim edges evenly. With tines of fork, score dough crosswise. Then, with sharp knife, cut crosswise into ¾-inch-wide strips.

Sand Tarts: Cut dough as for rounds, above. Cut out centers of half of rounds with small round or other shape aspic cutter. After baking, put one round and one cut-out cookie (lightly dusted with confectioners' sugar) together with raspberry or apricot jam.

Sandwich Cookies: After baking, put two cookies of the same shape together with a little jam.

To Decorate

To Decorate before Baking: Sprinkle the unbaked cookies with chopped walnuts, pistachios, or pecans, sliced almonds, chocolate shot, or candied cherries. Press the decorations lightly into cookies.

To Decorate after Baking: Dip ends of cookies in Chocolate Glaze; then dip ends in chopped nuts or chocolate shot.

Or spread or drizzle Chocolate Glaze over cookies; then sprinkle with chopped nuts.

Chocolate Glaze

1. Place ½ cup semisweet-chocolate pieces, 2 tablespoons butter or margarine, and 1 tablespoon light cream in top of double boiler. Melt over hot, not boiling, water, stirring occasionally, until smooth.

2. Let stand about 5 minutes. Then use as dip or frosting for cookies. If glaze becomes too stiff to drizzle, place over hot water again.